The Manchester *Union Leader* in New Hampshire Elections

**The University Press
of New England**

Sponsoring Institutions
Brandeis University
Clark University
Dartmouth College
University of New Hampshire
University of Rhode Island
University of Vermont

The Manchester *Union Leader* in New Hampshire Elections

Eric P. Veblen

The University Press of New England   Hanover, New Hampshire 1975

TO MY PARENTS

Acknowledgments

I am grateful to many people who assisted me in this study. The interviewees, both politicians and journalists, gave generously of their time and contributed much informal advice besides the actual interview material. Judge William R. Johnson deserves special thanks. David M. Kovenock assisted in various ways. My colleagues in the Department of Political Science of Vassar College provided helpful encouragement and advice; John Paul Ryan in particular made a number of useful suggestions about data analysis. At the same time, I must stress that the shortcomings of this study are my sole responsibility.

Rose H. Aszklar and her associates at the Business Guild of New Haven skillfully transcribed many of the 1967–68 interviews. Mildred S. Tubby was very helpful and patient in typing the manuscript. I am also indebted to David Horne for his sharp editing.

Finally, I am grateful for the financial assistance of the Woodrow Wilson National Fellowship Foundation and the Vassar College Faculty Committee on Research.

Poughkeepsie, N.Y.   E.P.V.
June 1974

Contents

Tables

Graphs

CHAPTER ONE

William Loeb and His Newspaper

In recent years publisher William Loeb and the Manchester *Union Leader* have achieved a measure of national fame—or perhaps "notoriety" would be a better word. Loeb's editorial pyrotechnics —they are colorful attempts to convince his readership that his right-wing view of politics is the correct perspective—regularly receive national publicity during New Hampshire's quadrennial, first-in-the-nation presidential primary; but Loeb occasionally explodes into the national political consciousness between elections as well.

Is there substance behind the fireworks? Do Loeb and the *Union Leader* have a substantial impact on New Hampshire politics? Is Loeb's reputation deserved? To answer such questions I decided to examine one key area of New Hampshire state politics: elections for governor and United States senator. Do candidates in gubernatorial and senatorial primaries and general elections take the *Union Leader* into account when planning their strategies and campaign activities? Or is the Loeb press not taken very seriously?

Although campaign strategies are the main focus of this study, I shall also examine evidence of *Union Leader* impact on the electorate. In the course of the latter endeavor I shall consider the newspaper's role in presidential primaries and general elections.

Fundamentally I view the politically vigorous *Union Leader*, which dominates newspaper circulation in New Hampshire, as an extreme case for the potential exercise of influence on election campaigns and outcomes. If newspapers do produce a significant impact on elections, such results should be evident in New Hampshire. If the *Union Leader* has little impact, perhaps the power of the press has been overestimated.

Publisher Loeb bought the Manchester *Union Leader* and the New Hampshire *Sunday News* on November 1, 1946. Both papers place a strong emphasis on politics in their news columns and editorials. The *Union Leader* carries frequent banner headlines on page one and the back page, as well as prominent front-page editorials signed by Loeb. Making extensive use of bold type and capital letters, these editorials are written in a colorful though colloquial style. Loeb often employs them to direct the reader's attention to back-page "skyline" feature articles on political subjects.

The *Union Leader's* editorial page is the first page of the second section, and these inside editorials also carry bold headlines. In another attempt to direct reader attention to them, Loeb employs a talented cartoonist whose work appears at the top of the editorial page (Loeb points out that it is rare for a newspaper of the size of the *Union Leader* to have its own cartoonist). The publisher's outlook on politics pervades the news columns as well as its editorials.

Militant anticommunism is a prominent element of Loeb's political views. The publisher, who once wrote that "the only good Communist is a dead Communist,"[1] claims to have penetrated the Communist Party some years ago and thus to have gained an inside view of how the communists operate. Loeb perceives the communist conspiracy as a dangerous threat to the United States, not only externally but domestically. During a 1965 controversy over a bill that would have barred "subversive" persons from using state facilities—the aim was to ban communists from speaking on state college and university campuses—Loeb described his view of how communists work in New Hampshire:

The Communists, in their secret cell meetings in the state, have drawn up a very thorough list of the various leaders in the com-

1. "Collapse at Columbia," *Union Leader* (May 13, 1968), p. 1.

munications media and in politics. A study has been made of
each one of their habits, their emotions and to what they react.
When the signal goes out from the Communist headquarters,
the dedicated Communists press the buttons. This activates the
secondary group, who are leaders most susceptible to Communist suggestions—although, of course, they are not Communists
themselves. The second group then goes into action and pretty
soon you have a mass uproar over a completely phony issue,
with the Communist dupes beating their breasts, believing that
this is all their own independent thinking and action. All the
while the Communists sit back and laugh their heads off at
what a silly bunch of people they have doing their work for
them.[2]

Loeb viewed Senator George McGovern (among other politicians) as a tool of the communist conspiracy:

Here we see the true picture of this man as the Communist candidate. If he should gain the White House, it is this newspaper's
belief that it would be a disaster to the nation. He would be the
first President of the United States to hold power with the
specific approval of the governments of Communist Russia
and Red China.

As readers of this newspaper are well aware, this writer once
penetrated the Communist Party without becoming a member
or working for the F.B.I. As a result, he well recognizes a man
that follows the Marxist line and a man who is willing to do the
bidding of the Communists. This writer believes that Senator
McGovern is such a man—the most dangerous man to ever run
for the presidency of the United States.[3]

Accordingly, Loeb favors aggressive anticommunist action abroad
and careful vigilance at home (in the 1950's he was a fervent sup-
porter of Senator Joseph McCarthy).
Loeb's outlook contains a stiff dose of ethnocentrism and reli-

2. "RED for the Republican Party; RED WHITE and BLUE for the Democratic Party," *Union Leader* (March 16, 1965), p. 1.
3. "Most Dangerous Man Ever to Run!" *Union Leader* (July 1, 1972), p. 1.

gious fundamentalism. In the past he has asserted that blacks are biologically inferior to whites[4] and that the civil rights movement is part of the communist conspiracy. He has called non-Christians and non-Jews—such as Buddhists and Muslims—"heathens" and "infidels."[5] Speaking of the North Vietnamese in 1969, Loeb asked: "How long is it going to be before the leaders of the American people—and the American people, themselves—realize that they are not up against a civilized foe? We are up against a ruthless group of savages, further heated up by the godless ideology of communism, which recognizes none of the concepts of Judaeo-Christian civilization such as mercy, charity and respect for life."[6]

Loeb is hardly reluctant to advocate the use of American military force in international relations, especially when dealing with non-Westerners. Reacting to the late-1973 Arab oil embargo, he urged President Nixon to warn the Arabs to halt the embargo OR ELSE:

> Then if these Arab dictators don't respond to this warning, there should be united military action by the countries of Europe, the United States and Japan to seize the oil and the oil production and keep the oil flowing to the industrial world. . . . One thing this newspaper can predict and that is if we sit around saying "pretty please" to these heathen swine we will get no oil and we will continue to suffer untold discomforts as well as great difficulty in maintaining our industrial production and our employment rolls. These desert satraps have lived by the sword so long they recognize only superior force.[7]

Except for the area of defense policy, Loeb tends to view the best government as the least government. He is a fiscal conservative and generally opposes governmental spending for domestic programs, whether at the national, state, or local level. He sees in-

4. "Protect the White Children," *Union Leader* (August 20, 1965), p. 1. The paper has not capitalized "Negro" in its news stories or editorials since August 1965.

5. For example, "Orientals Overlooked," *Union Leader* (January 25, 1966), p. 1.

6. "Retaliate Now!" *Union Leader* (March 7, 1969), p. 1.

7. "Let's Go after Our Oil," *Union Leader* (November 16, 1973).

creased spending as leading to higher taxes, which must be avoided at all costs. The staunch antitax position of the *Union Leader* is probably one reason why, as of mid-1974, New Hampshire is the only state with neither a general sales tax nor a general income tax.

The *Union Leader* publisher is alarmed at the growing permissiveness of society; several years ago he regularly labeled antiwar protesters "Spock-marked kids." Loeb's positions on such matters as race, law and order, protest activity, drugs, abortion, and what he regards as a general deterioration of values clearly mark him as a "Social Issue" conservative, to use Scammon and Wattenberg's term.[8] Rarely missing an opportunity to boost traditional moral and religious values and with a flag-waving brand of patriotism, he once commented: "As is well known to readers of this newspaper, this writer admires courage probably more than any other characteristic of human beings, next to loyalty."[9]

As a label of Loeb's political ideology, "conservative" serves well as a first approximation. Some of his ideas do not, however, fit the mold of a traditional conservative. For example, he favors labor unionism and has supported the repeal of Section 14-B of the Taft-Hartley Act, which allows the states to enact "right to work" legislation outlawing the union shop.[10] The *Union Leader* publisher is proud of his newspaper's profit-sharing arrangement and chides American businessmen for being short-sighted in not adopting profit-sharing on a widespread scale. Resenting the line of questioning by three reporters in a 1972 interview, he exclaimed:

8. Richard M. Scammon and Ben J. Wattenberg, *The Real Majority* (New York: Coward, McCann and Geoghegan, 1971), chapter 3.

9. "Courage," *Union Leader* (January 16, 1967), p. 1.

10. Loeb has long championed James R. Hoffa and the Teamsters Union, which loaned the Union Leader Corporation a total of over $2 million in 1963 and 1965: Helen Kirkpatrick Milbank, "New Hampshire's Paper Tiger," *Columbia Journalism Review*, 5 (1966), 11. It is interesting to note that Loeb's support of Hoffa did not begin until after the first Teamster loan to the newspaper—and that in fact the *Union Leader* had previously carried anti-Hoffa editorial material (see the issues of February 24, 1960; April 1, 1960; and August 12, 1960).

I am far more liberal than any of you are, because when I die
my papers are going to go to the people there. I share profits
now, I give them benefits that your employees never get—that
your fellow workers never get—and I'm just as much a liberal
and a believer in the best things for all the people in the United
States as you are. I'm getting damn tired of the supercilious attitude by some of you people who say, "Oh well, the *Union Leader*,
the *Union Leader*, it's a conservative reactionary paper." You
don't have any idea of what reactionary really is, and frankly,
you bore the hell out of me.[11]

Contrary to what we might expect from a conservative publisher,
Loeb speaks out against the trend toward monopoly ownership
of newspapers and against the ownership by newspapers of radio
and television stations in the same city. Loeb was one of the few
publishers who opposed the Newspaper Preservation Act, which
exempted newspapers from antitrust legislation in certain kinds of
joint operating arrangements.[12]

More generally, Loeb, who once called Nelson A. Rockefeller a
"spoiled rich kid,"[13] frequently engages in pro-working class, anti-
upper class rhetoric. A fairly typical example applied to state politics is the following excerpt from a 1972 editorial:

For a number of years, the Republican Party in New Hampshire has been controlled by a group of wealthy inheritors whose
locality is largely Concord, Peterborough and Dublin, New Hampshire. These people, it seems to this newspaper, fancy themselves
as THE people; you know, quite a few cuts above us ordinary
folks.

THE people go to the same preparatory schools. They generally go to many of the same Ivy League colleges. They go into
law and other professions and do rather well financially. There's
nothing wrong with that. In fact, we wish them every success.

The trouble starts when they think they have the right to

11. "William Loeb: 'I am far more liberal than you . . . ' " *Columbia Journalism Review*, 11 (1972), 22.
12. These views are elaborated in a letter to the members of the Forum for
Contemporary History, March 9, 1973.
13. "Rule-or-Ruin Rocky," *Union Leader* (November 20, 1963), p. 1.

control politics in New Hampshire and to impose their ideas on the rest of us. They seem to think that they should have control of political leadership in both political parties in the State of New Hampshire.[14]

Such appeals fit nicely the nature of Loeb's readership in Manchester, which is largely a working-class city. Several Loeb critics remarked to me that references to "us ordinary folks" and similar comments are ironic in view of the publisher's affluence (he lives in an estate in Prides Crossing, Massachusetts, and also has a home in Reno, Nevada).

Loeb's pro common-man rhetoric suggests that the label "populist" might be appropriate for his political views. And one can think of other ideological terms ("radical conservative"or "populistic conservative"). For convenience, however, I shall refer to Loeb in this book simply as a conservative—bearing in mind that he departs from traditional conservatism in several respects.

Leaving behind left-right ideological terminology, we might try to identify Loeb's fundamental view of politics. One basic theme in his editorials is a distrust of government, politics, and politicians. Government cannot be trusted to perform in the public interest. Politics is a sordid enterprise, and most politicians are corruptible if not corrupt. In general, they are dishonest— especially, it seems, the ones he opposes.

Among numerous examples is his 1963 accusation that President John F. Kennedy was the "number one liar in the United States."[15] In 1967 he charged that"[George] Romney is just a plain liar—and a STUPID liar, at that."[16] During the 1968 campaign he said in reference to two New Hampshire candidates he opposed, John W. King and Walter Peterson: "The truth is the truth and people who lie and deceive have no business in public office. . . . It is hard enough for the voters to pick a competent candidate for public office. Sometimes they vote for someone who *looks* pretty good

14. "Not only a Choice—but also a Chance!" *Union Leader* (September 25, 1972), p. 1.
15. "Number One Liar in the United States, John F. Kennedy," *Union Leader* (January 25, 1963), p. 1.
16. "Romney is THE Liar," *Union Leader* (July 27, 1967), p. 1.

and he turns out pretty sour afterwards, but at least they don't
have to start out by voting for men such as Peterson and King
who have indicated from the very outset that they will be less
than honest with the voters."[17] And after Thomas J. McIntyre
was re-elected senator in 1972, Loeb branded him a "vicious
damned liar."[18] Finally, Robert F. Kennedy received some of
the publisher's strongest criticism, as shown by these three statements from 1965, 1966, and 1968:

> In the opinion of this newspaper, Bobby Kennedy is the most
> vicious and most dangerous political leader in the United States
> today.[19]

> In our estimation, Bobby Kennedy is the most vicious and
> dangerous political leader ever to appear on the U.S. scene.[20]

> Bobby Kennedy is no Jack Kennedy. In the estimation of this
> newspaper he is one of the most ruthless men who ever trod
> the face of this earth.[21]

Although distrust of politicians is Loeb's usual message, he can
be euphoric about public figures he admires. For example, in a
1964 front-page editorial entitled "Of the People, For the People,
By the People," he wrote this passage concerning the Goldwater
campaign: "This is a holy crusade against those who have stolen
the birthright of America, your birthright and that of every citizen
of the United States. No one is too humble or too great to join this
battle, no one can do too little or too much. Everything and everybody should help, if we are to save our beloved nation."[22] Goldwater—as well as several New Hampshire figures, including Governor
Meldrim Thomson, Jr., and the late Senator Styles Bridges—was an
exception to Loeb's rule that politicians are untrustworthy.

17. "Come Up out of the Mud, Governor!" *Union Leader* (October 30,
1968), p. 1.
18. "McIntyre Is a Vicious Damned Liar!" *Union Leader* (November 17,
1972), p. 1.
19. "Bar Bobby!" *Union Leader* (November 10, 1965), p. 1.
20. "Yorty Discovers the Real Bobby," *Union Leader* (September 9,
1966), p. 1.
21. "The American Dictator," *Union Leader* (March 20, 1968), p. 1.
22. "Of the People, for the People, by the People," *Union Leader* (February 17, 1964), p. 1.

The examples demonstrate that Loeb has a basically conspiratorial view of politics, in which the forces of good are constantly engaged in a struggle with the forces of evil. Important political questions are black and white.

In October 1967 I made the first of two visits to Loeb's Massachusetts estate. During that interview (the second was in March 1973) Loeb made it clear that he pictures himself as a throwback to such controversial, old-time publishers as William Randolph Hearst. Above all, he strives to make the *Union Leader* interesting to read. He claims that American newspapers today shy away from controversy in order to avoid making enemies, and in the process become insufferably dull. According to him, most publishers think they will make more money by avoiding controversy; but this approach backfires because a colorful paper will sell more copies than a dull one.[23] At least this is his theory, and he puts it into practice with the *Union Leader*. Dramatic conflicts and controversies are sought rather than avoided. For example, when a politician criticizes Loeb, the publisher frequently prints the politician's statement on the front page together with an attack on him by Loeb. The *Leader's* readable layout is another attempt to make the paper interesting and exciting.

As part of the endeavor to attract readers, Loeb likes to present political content in emotional terms. Political news that cannot be easily simplified and personified (the good guys against the bad guys) runs the risk of being omitted or buried in the *Leader's* inside pages. A Concord lawyer remarked to me, "I don't think Loeb's whole approach fits with trying to inform the people about complicated problems that don't have a high emotional content."[24]

Most of the New Hampshire newspapermen I interviewed, having stated that a publisher should have the freedom to publish his paper as he sees fit, went on to express varying degrees of disdain toward Loeb's approach to publishing. For example, regarding Loeb's style of personal journalism, Keene *Sentinel* publisher James D. Ewing stated:

> I have no quarrel with that. I don't happen to believe in it myself, but I think that the style with which anyone runs a paper is a

23. Interview October 23, 1967.
24. Interview with Charles F. Leahy, August 23, 1972.

matter of his own personal taste. . . . My quarrels with the *Union Leader* as a newspaper don't rest on that at all. They rest on the fact that I think while in many respects it's an admirable newspaper, when it comes to politics or politically oriented issues, it very often blurs the line between news and editorial views; and I just don't think this is good newspapering.[25]

Including a morning edition distributed statewide and an evening edition for Manchester, the *Union Leader* has a circulation of 64,000. This figure may not sound large, but it is almost 40 percent of the total circulation of all daily newspapers published in New Hampshire and is almost three times that of the second-largest paper.[26] Moreover, the *Union Leader* is the only paper distributed throughout the state.

The Loeb press faces a degree of political competition from the evening dailies. Throughout most of the past decade, five of these papers took generally moderate editorial positions which frequently opposed the stands of the *Union Leader.*[27] Two other dailies were conservative and usually supported the same issue positions and candidates as the Loeb press.[28] One other paper rarely became politically involved.[29]

Besides circulation dominance, the virtual absence of New Hampshire television stations helps potential *Leader* influence. The bulk of the TV reception is from Boston channels, which cover the heavily populated southern part of New Hampshire. The state's single VHF commercial station (located in Manchester) must compete against a fellow ABC affiliate in Boston.[30] The Massachusetts stations carry very little news of New Hampshire politics, and their advertising rates are too high for candidates in New Hampshire gubernatorial and senatorial campaigns. Some parts of the state receive television broadcasts from Vermont and

25. Interview, September 8, 1967.
26. *Editor and Publisher International Year Book*, 1973.
27. Claremont *Eagle*, Concord *Monitor*, Keene *Sentinel*, Lebanon *Valley News*, and Portsmouth *Herald*.
28. Dover *Foster's Democrat* and Nashua *Telegraph*.
29. Laconia *Citizen*.
30. New Hampshire also has one UHF commercial station (Lebanon) and one UHF public station (Durham).

Maine, but again not much New Hampshire political news comes from these sources. Thus it is likely that New Hampshire residents obtain much less information about state politics from television than do citizens of most other states. This weakness of television magnifies the importance of a high-circulation newspaper like the *Union Leader.*

New Hampshire is a rapidly growing state whose population increased by 22 percent during the 1960's to reach the 1970 total of almost 738,000.[31] Most of this growth took place in the dynamic southern part of New Hampshire, which accounts for the bulk of the state's population. I estimate that in 1970, 61 percent of New Hampshirites lived within 25 miles of the Massachusetts border (this figure might be off by one or two percentage points). This southern area accounted for 77 percent of the state's total net population increase from 1960 to 1970.

New Hampshire has no really big cities (Manchester is the largest, with a 1970 population of about 88,000) and few large industries. The state, however, has a long tradition of small manufacturing concerns. Textiles and leather goods dominated in the nineteenth century, but a wide variety of products are produced today. Only four states have a larger percentage of population employed in manufacturing industries.[32]

The state is racially homogeneous, with a nonwhite population of only 0.6 percent.[33] On the other hand, there is a degree of ethnic heterogeneity. As we shall see below, the mixture of sizable Franco-American and Irish populations with the traditional Yankee stock has produced significant political implications.

During the long period of Republican dominance which began after the Civil War, New Hampshire Democrats consistently polled a respectable share of the vote but just as consistently failed to win gubernatorial and senatorial elections (notable exceptions were Democratic gubernatorial victories in 1912 and 1922, and a U.S.

31. U.S. Census figures reprinted in the *State of New Hampshire Manual for the General Court, 1973* (Concord: Department of State), pp. 274-290.
32. Bureau of the Census, *Census of Population: 1970. General Social and Economic Characteristics*, Final Report, United States Summary, Table 141.
33. Ibid., *Census of Population: 1970. General Population Characteristics*, Final Report, New Hampshire, Table 18.

Senate triumph in 1932. In recent years, however, there has been a
striking turnabout in Democratic fortunes.

New Hampshire Democrats came fairly close to winning the
governorship several times in the 1950's. In 1954 and 1956 their
candidate received 45 percent of the vote, despite the Eisenhower
landslide in the latter year.[34] In 1958 a group of young Democratic
insurgents, who had been battling the more traditional, patronage-
oriented elements in their party for several years, succeeded in
nominating Bernard L. Boutin for the governorship. Boutin waged
a strong campaign and garnered 48 percent of the vote against
Republican Wesley Powell. A 1960 rematch between Boutin and
Powell found Democratic hopes very high, especially with Massachusetts neighbor John F. Kennedy heading the ticket. Boutin,
however, won only 44 percent of the vote in that election.

The Democratic breakthrough came in 1962 with the help of a
severe split in the Republican Party. Governor Powell lost a bitter
primary against John Pillsbury and strongly supported Democratic
candidate John W. King in the general election. King won in a
landslide with 59 percent of the vote. The same year Democrat
Thomas J. McIntyre (52 percent) was elected to the Senate seat
of the late Styles Bridges, who had died in November 1961. McIntyre
defeated Congressman Perkins Bass, who had won a bitter primary
battle against three other major candidates, including Senator
Bridges' widow Doloris. Neither King nor McIntyre faced significant opposition in the primary and thus carried a relatively unified
party into the general election. Aided by the 1964 Johnson sweep,[35]
King won reelection with 67 percent of the vote. In 1966 both King
and McIntyre won with 54 percent. Thus the long-unsuccessful
Democrats retained the governor's chair and one of the U.S. Senate
seats.

The tables turned in 1968, however. Governor King decided to
challenge incumbent Senator Norris Cotton and was beaten badly.
Meanwhile, Republican Speaker of the House Walter Peterson
took over the governor's chair. A moderate, Peterson won a close
primary over former Governor Powell and conservative newcomer
Meldrim Thomson, Jr. The Republican nominee went on to defeat

34. See the biennial volumes of the *State of New Hampshire Manual for the
General Court* (Concord: Department of State).
35. L.B.J. carried New Hampshire with 64 percent of the vote.

Democrat Emile R. Bussiere by a fairly comfortable margin (53 percent to 47 percent).

The Republican Party retained the governorship in the 1970 and 1972 elections, but only after hotly contested primaries. In 1970 Governor Peterson edged Thomson in a close primary and barely slipped by Democratic nominee Roger J. Crowley, Jr., in the general election; Peterson tallied 46 percent to Crowley's 44 percent, while Thomson, running under the banner of the American Party, won 10 percent. In 1972 Thomson, once again a Republican, finally beat Peterson in another close primary. Thomson then edged Crowley and moderate Republican Malcolm McLane, running as an independent, in the general election; Thomson won 41 percent of the vote, Crowley 39 percent, and McLane 20 percent.

Although the Democrats failed to win back the governorship, Senator McIntyre gained reelection in 1972. McIntyre swamped that perennial candidate, former Governor Powell, in a 57-to-43 landslide.

Meanwhile Republican Congressmen James C. Cleveland and Louis C. Wyman have established a firm hold on New Hampshire's two seats in the United States House of Representatives. First elected in 1962, both Cleveland and Wyman had problems in the 1964 Goldwater debacle. Cleveland barely escaped defeat, but Wyman was beaten by Democrat J. Oliva Huot. In 1966 Wyman rejoined Cleveland in the House by winning a rematch over Huot. In 1970 and 1972 both Republican congressmen won by better than two-to-one margins.

Although the Democrats are hardly New Hampshire's dominant party, their recent successes have made them a threat in gubernatorial and senatorial elections. One demographic trend which apparently has favored the Democratic Party is the rapid population increase in southern New Hampshire. Much of this growth is accounted for by Massachusetts Democrats who have moved across the border. Dishman and Ford have shown that in one southeastern New Hampshire county the towns with the largest increase in number of voters from 1950 to 1960 also had the greatest increase in Democratic voting strength.[36] Both the Democrats and the Republicans have had difficulty capitalizing on

36. Robert B. Dishman and Joseph P. Ford, "The New Hampshire Party System, 1968" (University of New Hampshire, 1968, mimeographed), p. 9A.

these recent arrivals. Many of these people continue to work in
Massachusetts, watch Boston television, and for all practical purposes remain political citizens of Massachusetts with no interest
in New Hampshire politics.

Despite the various Democratic victories since 1960, New
Hampshire remains basically a Republican state (though not by
a large margin). The Democrats have been unable to win control
of either branch of the state legislature (the General Court).
Dishman and Ford argue, moreover, that New Hampshire's underlying partisan distribution remained almost constant from 1890 to
1966. Using off-year elections for the Governor's Council (a state
office) as an indicator of normal party strength, these authors show
that during this period Democratic candidates consistently gathered
around 45 percent of the total state vote for the office.[37] This
pattern held for 1970 as well.[38]

In order to succeed, Democratic gubernatorial and senatorial
candidates must attract a good number of normally Republican
voters and independents. One way to do this is to take advantage
of splits within the Republican Party. Once in office, Democratic
incumbents are in a position to consolidate their support and may
be formidable candidates in subsequent elections—as demonstrated
by Senator McIntyre and former Governor King.

In the past the main social bases of cleavage between New Hampshire Democrats and Republicans have been ethnic, religious, and
occupational factors. Democrats have been disporportionately
Franco-Americans or Irish, Catholics, and blue-collar workers.
Republicans, on the other hand, have tended to be Yankees, Prot-
estants, and farmers or professionals. Writing in 1959, Lockard
offers empirical evidence for these generalizations. For cities with
a population of at least 5,000, he calculated the following strong
rank-order correlations with percent Democratic in the 1954 guber-

37. Ibid., p. 14A.
38. The Democratic candidates captured only 39 percent of the vote in
1970, but one of the five Governor's Council seats was uncontested that
year. Using a procedure analogous to that employed by Dishman and Ford,
I substituted the 1966 vote in that district for the 1970 value. If this sub-
stitution is made, the total statewide vote for Democrats was 43 percent in
1970.

natorial election: percent foreign born, .74; percent French Cana-
dian born, .87; and percent employed in manufacturing, .92.[39]

In order to bring Lockard's figures closer to the present, I
examined the 1970 gubernatorial election for the same twelve
cities considered by Lockard, and calculated the following Spear-
man rank-order correlations with percent Democratic in that
election: percent foreign born, .54; percent of foreign-stock
population originating from Canada, .12; and percent employed
in manufacturing, .38. These correlations become, respectively,
.42, .39, and .71 if the home city of the Democratic candidate
(Manchester) is excluded.[40] Thus it appears that the traditional
social distinctions between New Hampshire Democrats and Republicans have begun to fade away during the past two decades—though
these old social cleavages are still noticeable.

The state's Democrats appear to be somewhat more liberal than
the Republicans, but one must be careful not to exaggerate the
ideological or policy-position difference. A systematic public
opinion survey conducted in February 1968 suggests that self-
identified Republicans are more conservative than the Democrats
on several questions dealing with the intervention of the federal
government in economic, educational, and civil-rights matters.
For example, one question asked, "Do you think the Government
in Washington should see to it that every person has a job and a
good standard of living, or should it let each person get ahead on
his own?" Examining only respondents who stated that they intended to vote in the 1968 presidential primary, we find that 15
percent of the Republicans and 39 percent of the Democrats
selected the response, "The Government in Washington should
help"; 78 percent of the Republicans and 55 percent of the Democrats agreed that the Government should "Let each get ahead on his
own" (7 percent of the Republicans and 6 percent of the Democrats

39. Duane Lockard, *New England State Politics* (Princeton: Princeton University Press, 1959), p. 64.
40. The country-of-origin information was not available for two of the
cities, so the two corresponding correlations (.12 and .39) are based on ten
and nine cases respectively. My source for the socio-economic data: Bureau
of the Census, *Census of Population: 1970. General Social and Economic
Characteristics*, Final Report, New Hampshire, Tables 81, 87, 102, 106, 117.

said they did not know, or gave no answer).[41] The Democrats do appear to be the more liberal group.

On the other hand, this conclusion does not necessarily hold true for state issues such as taxes. Moreover, voters do not necessarily choose among statewide candidates primarily on the basis of ideology or policy preference. Nevertheless, it is plausible that on the whole, New Hampshire Democrats are somewhat more liberal than Republicans in state politics.

In this century intraparty ethnic competition has been a handicap for New Hampshire Democrats and helped to prolong Republican dominance. The Franco American versus Irish rivalry became particularly bitter in the 1930's and blood-letting primary battles worked to the advantage of the Republicans in the general elections.[42] The intensity of this ethnic competition has since subsided but remains an important cleavage within the Democratic Party. An indication of the influence of ethnicity on voting patterns is provided by Lockard's examination of the 1954 Democratic senatorial primary, which pitted a Franco American against an Irishman. The (rank order?) correlation between the percentage of Franco Americans in a town and that town's vote for the Franco-American candidate was .82 (omitting the candidates' home towns).[43]

In recent years (especially since the Eugene McCarthy campaign in the 1968 Democratic presidential primary) an ideological cleavage has become more pronounced within the Democratic party. It is risky to try to separate this ideological or policy division from other factors, but I think it would be safe to say that in state politics the more conservative Democratic voters outnumber the more liberal Democrats. This proposition is certainly plausible in view of the 1970 and 1972 Democratic gubernatorial primary victories of moderate conservative Roger Crowley, who won by substantial margins both times over more liberal opponents.

The Republican Party has not experienced the ethnic cleavages

41. Austin Ranney, "Turnout and Representation in Presidential Primary Elections," *American Political Science Review*, 66 (1972), 30.

42. A history of Democratic Party factionalism can be found in William L. Dunfey, "A Short History of the Democratic Party in New Hampshire" (unpublished M.A. thesis, University of New Hampshire, 1954).

43. Lockard, p. 67.

that have plagued the Democrats. Although it is difficult to trace
well-defined Republican factions, I (and New Hampshire politicians) find it useful to view the Republican electorate on a moder-
ate-to-conservative continuum. This image of the party does not
imply that most voters think ideologically, but rather that they
are consistently attracted to candidates who can meaningfully
be labeled as more or less conservative. Of course, some candidates
defy simple classification in these terms. The outcomes of recent
primary elections suggest that the Republican Party is evenly
divided between the more moderate and more conservative sides.

In an attempt to investigate the persistence of ideological factions in the Republican Party, I examined the votes for the more
conservative candidates in the 1960 and 1972 gubernatorial primaries; these candidates were, respectively, Wesley Powell and
Meldrim Thomson. If persistent ideological factions existed from
1960 to 1972, one would expect Powell and Thomson to have run
most strongly in the same areas of New Hampshire. Using the procedure employed in Chapter 5, below, I correlated the votes for
Powell (1960) and Thomson (1972) in the state's ten counties.
The resulting product-moment correlation for the counties is
.34. The correlation for the six counties which were the homes of
no candidates in either election is .72.

One must beware of applying this technique to the present case.
There were considerable changes in population between 1960 and
1972. Even in the absence of such movement, if the same county
delivers exactly the same percentage of the vote to two candidates
in two different elections, the same *individuals* do not necessarily
vote the same way both times; so we must beware of drawing
conclusions for individual voters, as opposed to aggregates of
voters. The number of cases is very small, especially for the "non-
home" county correlation. And finally, Powell is one of those
candidates whose appeal transcends ideological boundaries, so
it may be dangerous to place him in the same category as other
conservatives.

With these caveats in mind, I decided to apply the same technique to consecutive elections, the 1966 Republican senatorial
primary and the 1968 Republican gubernatorial primary. The most
conservative candidates in these elections were, respectively,

Harrison R. Thyng and again Thomson. For all ten counties the
product-moment correlation between the Thyng vote (1966) and
the Thomson vote (1968) is .47—and .61 for the five "non-home"
counties (this number of cases is really too small for the correlation value to be very meaningful).

The foregoing data provide a small amount of support to the
hypothesis that ideological groups of Republican voters persist
over time. Although the figures do not clearly contradict this
theory, the relationships are not so strong as we might have expected.

Neither the Democrats nor the Republicans have powerful, cohesive party organizations. There is no strong party "machine" able
to discipline dissident members. Fragmentation among party
leaders, not unity, is the common state of affairs. From time to
time certain individuals are able to build strong personal organizations within a party. The most prominent example in recent
decades was the late Senator Styles Bridges, several of whose
protégés achieved political prominence in their own right (for
example, former Governor Powell and Congressman Wyman).
But cohesive personal organizations like Bridges' have been rare
and are obviously not the same thing as official party organizations.

In both the Democratic and Republican parties, the institution
of the primary election has worked against party unity. Candidates
are able to succeed by appealing directly to the voters rather than
by placing top priority on cooperation with party leaders. In
addition to the *existence* of the primary election, the *timing* of the
primary facilitates intraparty factionalism and disunity. The primary is held in the first half of September, a situation that produces a relatively long primary campaign (often lasting at least
six months) and a fairly short general election campaign (no more
than two months). There is thus plenty of time to open wounds
in a bruising primary fight but little time to heal these wounds and
unite the party for the general election. The absence of a run-off
primary allows a candidate to win with a minority of the votes and
might possibly retard the coalition-building process prior to the
fall campaign. Throughout the entire primary process, the *Union
Leader's* flaming rhetoric has an explosive rather than a soothing
effect on intraparty antagonisms.

In view of the impact of the *Union Leader* on New Hampshire
politics, the political nature of Manchester is an important consideration. The individuals I interviewed uniformly characterized Manchester as a generally conservative city, most of whose residents
might be expected to sympathize with Loeb's political views (at
least his less extreme ones). Although socioeconomic variables are
only imperfectly related to political behavior, several statistics
from the 1970 census shed some light on the nature of Manchester.
A minority of the city's workers (44 percent) are employed in
white-collar occupations, and the median family income of $9489
falls below the national figure of $9590. Thirty-four percent of the
workers are employed in manufacturing industries, and 41 percent
of the children in elementary school attend private school (a rough
indicator of the percentage of Catholics).[44] Manchester appears to
be not an overly prosperous city (though not especially poor
either) with a substantial industrial, working-class population and a
fairly large proportion of Catholic citizens. It is not surprising that
Manchester is solidly Democratic. Moreover, one might speculate
that if the city's residents are conservative, they are less economic
conservatives than "Social Issue" conservatives. All in all, the
picture is not unpromising for Loeb's populistic-style appeals.

The political importance of the Manchester area is demonstrated
by the size of its vote in various types of New Hampshire elections.
The highest per-capita *Union Leader* circulation is in the "Manchester city zone" (as defined by the Audit Bureau of Circulations),
consisting of Manchester and the contiguous suburbs of Auburn,
Bedford, Goffstown, Hooksett, and Londonderry. In recent
gubernatorial and senatorial elections the Manchester city zone
has accounted for somewhat more than one third of the statewide
vote in Democratic primaries; somewhat more than one tenth in
Republican primaries; and somewhat less than one fifth in general

44. Bureau of the Census, *Census of Population: 1970. General Social and
Economic Characteristics*, Final Report, United States Summary, Tables 83,
186, 187.
45. The exact percentages run as follows:

1960 Democratic gubernatorial primary	37
1960 Democratic senatorial primary	39
1970 Democratic gubernatorial primary	39

elections. These figures appear not to have changed since 1960.[45]

Before examining the impact of the *Union Leader* on campaign strategies, I should warn that this study excludes paid advertising. The rationale for the restriction is that advertising is a relatively automatic process as far as a newspaper is concerned; the candidate pays his money and places his ad. In news stories and editorials, on the other hand, newspaper personnel are active participants in determining the nature of the stories that are printed.

Most of my interviews (described more fully in Appendix B) were conducted in 1967 and 1972. I concentrate on the period from 1960 to 1972, a manageable time span which had not completely faded from the memories of the interviewees.

1972 Democratic gubernatorial primary	36
1960 Republican gubernatorial primary	13
1970 Republican gubernatorial primary	12
1972 Republican gubernatorial primary	12
1972 Republican senatorial primary	13
1960 Gubernatorial general election	18
1960 Senatorial general election	18
1970 Gubernatorial general election	19
1972 Gubernatorial general election	16
1972 Senatorial general election	16

CHAPTER TWO

The 1966 Senate Campaigns

The 1966 Republican primary and general election to select a United States senator from New Hampshire will serve to illustrate the strategic impact of the *Union Leader* in the recent past. We will be concerned with two types of strategic calculations by candidates: deciding whether to run in the first place, and selecting a principal campaign strategy. With respect to the latter category, of special interest will be decisions about the handling of issues during the campaign. Did the candidates take the *Union Leader* into account in their calculations? If the newspaper was considered, did it actually influence candidates' decisions? In other words, would the candidates have acted differently in the absence of the *Union Leader*?

The Republican Senatorial Primary

Democratic Senator Thomas J. McIntyre had been elected in 1962 with the aid of a sharp split in Republican ranks. Nineteen sixty-six looked like a Republican year, and McIntyre appeared to be vulnerable. The coveted GOP nomination attracted the attention of numerous potential Republican primary candidates.

William Loeb's Manchester *Union Leader* and New Hampshire *Sunday News* had been consistent and strong critics of Senator McIntyre. In 1965 the Loeb press, particularly the *Sunday News* and its editor, B. J. McQuaid, began a search for a candidate who could defeat McIntyre. In May and June several prominently displayed stories appeared concerning the possibility that astronaut Alan Shepard, a New Hampshire native, might be interested in running for the Senate. Page one of the June 13 *Sunday News* carried a letter from McQuaid to Shepard urging the latter to run. Shortly thereafter the astronaut announced that he preferred to remain in the space program rather than enter the political arena.

Several months later a new possible candidate began to appear in print. Two September 10 editorials suggested the need for the GOP to tap fresh political talent, and complimented forty-six year old General Harrison R. Thyng, "New Hampshire's number one wartime ace," for a speech blasting anti-Vietnam war protesters.[1] In late November an editorial and news-story publicity buildup for General Thyng began in earnest. A page one banner headline in the November 28th *Sunday News* proclaimed, " 'Thyng for U.S. Senate,' " and the article asserted that many New Hampshireites were urging the General to declare himself a candidate. Occasional news stories and favorable editorials about Thyng appeared throughout the following two months. A well-publicized announcement on January 31 by Thyng's brother, Charles Thyng, stated that the General intended to retire from the Air Force and run for the Senate. By February 1966 it was obvious that Thyng was a candidate and that he would have *Union Leader* backing. A February 3 Concord *Monitor* editorial placed Thyng in "the Loeb stable of candidates."[2]

To what extent did the Loeb press encourage General Thyng to run for the Senate and thus recruit the candidate? Stories circulated by former Governor Wesley Powell in late 1965 claimed that the Thyng candidacy was being planned in a series of "secret meetings" at William Loeb's home in Prides Crossing, Massachusetts.[3] A version of this rumor holds that at least one meeting was attended by Texas oilman H. L. Hunt, who agreed to help line up financial support for the Thyng campaign. Another version reports that such a meeting was held early in the summer and that Alan Shepard was selected as a possible candidate. The *Sunday News*, though, denied such stories: "Actually no such meetings as the ones Powell described ever took place although on one recent occasion

1. "G.O.P. at the Crossroads" and "War Ace Lashes Beatniks," *Union Leader* (September 10, 1965).
2. "The Campaign Is On," *Monitor* (February 3, 1966).
3. " 'Thyng for U.S. Senate' " *Sunday News*, (November 28, 1965), p. 1.

General Thyng did pay a social call on Mr. and Mrs. Loeb."[4] Supporters of the theory that Loeb helped to recruit Thyng say it was an open secret that *Sunday News* editor B. J. McQuaid flew to Goose Bay, Labrador, while Thyng was stationed there in late 1965, in order to convince him to run.

Whatever encouragement he received from the Loeb newspapers, General Thyng had been considering a plunge into politics. In the interview he observed that by running for public office he sacrificed continued military service and the benefits obtained from reaching the top of that profession. But he was so concerned about the state of world affairs and American policies that he decided to run anyway.[5]

Loeb support may not have been the key to Thyng's decision, but whether the General realized it or not, *Union Leader* backing was necessary for him to become a serious threat for the nomination. It is highly unlikely, for example, that Thyng could have made a strong showing if Alan Shepard or somebody else had run with Loeb's endorsement. It seems probable that if the *Union Leader* had actively supported another candidate, Thyng would not have entered the race. At any rate, on March 25, 1966, he formally announced his candidacy for the United States Senate. His resignation from the Air Force became effective April 1.

The second declared candidate was William R. Johnson. A thirty-five year old Hanover lawyer, Johnson was the State Senate majority leader and had been Republican party chairman since early 1965. Though he had thoughts of eventually running for higher office, Johnson did not initially intend to become a senatorial candidate in 1966. He tried in 1965 to find one moderate "non-Loeb" Republican who would agree to run for the Senate, with the promise that as state chairman he would wage a vigorous campaign for the candidate. Johnson wanted a nominee to emerge from the 1966 primary who could win the general election, and he felt that a conservative supported by the *Union Leader* could not defeat Senator McIntyre. Moreover, as a moderate-liberal Republican who had worked for Rockefeller in 1964 and who was on

4. Ibid.
5. Interview with Harrison R. Thyng, August 15, 1967. General Thyng declined to have his interview quoted directly.

record against a major bill to ban communist speakers from college campuses, Johnson felt that retention of his job as state party chairman depended on a moderate's winning the nomination. In Johnson's mind, William Loeb was a force to consider:

> It was perfectly obvious that if Loeb were ever to nominate a candidate or have control of the nominating process, he would insist upon a state chairman who was ideologically at least acceptable to Loeb. He would either have to be someone who has no "ideology" or he would have to be somebody who was a Goldwater type of conservative. I sure as hell wouldn't fit. . . . Consequently there wasn't any doubt that if Loeb ever gained control through the nominating process of even one candidate, I'd be out.[6]

As *Union Leader* support for Harry Thyng picked up in early 1966, Johnson increased his efforts to induce a moderate to run. However, the several potential candidates approached by the state chairman refused to commit themselves to making a race. Convinced that an opponent against Thyng had to announce soon, Johnson decided in early April to become a candidate himself. He thought that his chances of winning the nomination were small but were more attractive than what he felt would be his certain ouster as party chairman if Thyng did not meet opposition in the near future. Thus William Loeb and the *Union Leader* played a part in Johnson's decision to run.

Having decided to enter the race, Johnson thought that he needed two things to happen if he were going to have a chance. First, other moderate candidates had to stay out for a while in order to allow Johnson to establish himself as the front-running opponent to Thyng. As a relatively little-known political newcomer, Johnson was especially concerned with the need to establish an early lead over other candidates. The possible entrants who most worried Johnson were National Committeeman and former Congressman Perkins Bass and former Governor Lane Dwinell, who was a special threat because his home was near Johnson's.

According to Johnson's strategic calculations, the second necessary event was an editorial attack on him by William Loeb

6. Interview with William R. Johnson, July 31, 1967.

in the *Union Leader.* Johnson felt that an immediate blast by
Loeb would help considerably by giving the candidate publicity
and visibility: "Loeb had to attack me to make me a newsworthy
item."[7] Moreover, Johnson felt that an early Loeb attack would
help him win the sympathy of "the voters in this state who are
knee-jerk reactionaries to Loeb, who so completely negatively react
to what he says that they are for you if he's against you." Johnson
estimated that between five and ten percent of the electorate fell
into this anti-Loeb category.

Finally, a very important reason for Johnson's wanting a Loeb
attack was that he felt it would help him pick up the editorial
support of other newspapers—backing he called "absolutely critical," especially for voter support. Johnson, planning to respond to
Loeb's blast with a blistering attack on the *Union Leader* publisher,
reasoned that once he became known as a candidate openly fighting
against Loeb, most editors (being unfavorably disposed to Loeb)
would be interested in meeting Johnson: "Rather than giving you
a fifteen-minute courtesy call, they give you half an hour to an
hour and let you if you can do it have a chance to impress them
with your intelligence and knowledge, etc. . . . You sold yourself
because you had a hearing, but you got the hearing because you
made the statement about Loeb."

Johnson planned systematically how to deal with the anticipated Loeb blast:

> This is his standard operating procedure, which I had followed
> over a period of years. I'd studied every campaign, and I recog-
> nized that this was going to be the Loeb treatment; and I
> relied upon it as being an essential element. I had written in my
> own mind—I even had some brief notes on the press conference
> that I was going to hold on Friday after I was being attacked on
> Thursday. I hadn't even announced yet; but in my mind I had
> seen the attack and seen the response and even had thought
> through how I should respond and what I should do and the
> format of the response and the idea of calling a press conference.
> And the whole thing I had worked out in my own mind as being

7. Ibid. The Johnson quotes in the following paragraphs are taken from
the same interview.

the essential step-by-step analysis, as being critical in order to sustain the campaign.

In short, as he prepared to announce his candidacy, Johnson anticipated the necessity for other moderates to stay out of the race in the near future and for Loeb to criticize him strongly: "An absolutely critical break-off point in my decision tree was a Loeb attack. Had Loeb not attacked me or had Perkins Bass or Lane Dwinell or one of those candidates jumped in shortly there-after, I was prepared to spend half as much money just to run an exciting campaign but not a well financed campaign."

Monday, April 11, Johnson presided at the annual meeting of the Republican State Committee in Concord. He had hoped to delay his declaration as a candidate until some time after this "unity" meeting, but news had leaked out that he planned to enter. So the following morning Johnson announced his candidacy at a Concord press conference. He declared that he would offer the voters a "choice" and complimented General Thyng as "a man of high intelligence and integrity." Johnson also promised to give Thyng his "whole-hearted support" if the General should win the primary. Johnson's statement made no mention of William Loeb.[8]

The anticipated Loeb attack appeared two mornings later in a *Union Leader* front-page editorial titled "Ridiculous!" Loeb asserted that Johnson had improperly used the Republican state chairmanship to build himself up as a candidate. The publisher stated that Johnson had "no qualifications" to serve in the Senate and ridiculed the idea of having two senators from the same law firm (Johnson was at the time a law partner of Senator Norris Cotton, though Johnson shortly resigned from the firm). Loeb ended: "The only people opposing Harry Thyng in New Hampshire are the left wing, anti-God, anti-patriotism newspaper publishers and the usual Ivy League eggheads, who are in favor of world government and appeasement."[9]

The following morning Johnson unleased his barrage at Loeb. Citing the publisher's divisive effect on the Republican Party, Johnson asserted that "Mr. Loeb has made himself an issue" and stated, "Because of his devastating effect on political life in this

8. "Johnson Joins Senate Race," *Union Leader* (April 13, 1966), p. 1.
9. "Ridiculous!" *Union Leader* (April 14, 1966), p. 1.

State, I believe each candidate must take a stand on the issue of Mr. Loeb. My own position is that the Republican Party should, once and for all time, reject him and his brand of politics."[10]

This was the kind of controversy which delights the *Union Leader* owner. In a page one story that included Johnson's statement, Loeb replied:

> I hope Mr. Johnson will forgive me if I say that my first reaction was to recall the words of a famous Democratic politician, former President Harry Truman, who once said: "If you can't stand the heat, get the hell out of the kitchen." Candidate Johnson's excited reaction to our mild editorial of Wednesday would seem to indicate that he can't even stand the heat from a toaster at the breakfast table.[11]

Loeb also questioned who was behind the campaign to beat General Thyng. Johnson's hoped-for confrontation with Loeb had indeed occurred.

The early stages of the campaign went well for Johnson. Other "moderate" candidates stayed out of the race, and for three months Johnson and Thyng were the only announced Republican senatorial contestants. As part of his attempt to keep unwanted competitors from entering soon, Johnson campaigned vigorously and unleashed an early flurry of advertising. He tried to convince potential opposition that he was a serious candidate who was willing to spend a fair amount of money.

At the same time, Johnson was satisfied with the press reaction to his argument with Loeb. A number of newspapers complimented the Hanover Republican for openly confronting the *Union Leader* publisher, Portsmouth *Herald* editor Richard Blalock writing an especially hard-hitting editorial. The Concord *Monitor* commented: "Johnson, to his credit, is the first candidate for major office in this state who has dared stand up to the down river publisher [Loeb]."[12]

Johnson's second major confrontation took place in late April

10. "Johnson Issues Loeblast," *Monitor* (April 15, 1966), p. 1.

11. "Loeb Editorial Sparks Joust with Johnson," *Union Leader* (April 16, 1966), p. 1.

12. "Johnson Has Loeb Ducking and Dodging," *Monitor* (April 28, 1966).

over his alleged suppression of a "secret poll" he had taken as
state chairman in 1965; a split front-page story on April 27 carried
a Johnson charge and a Loeb response. The results of this argument
were inconclusive but gave Johnson another chance to exchange
barbs in public with the publisher. The lead paragraph of a May 1st
page one *Sunday News* story exemplifies the kind of coverage
that was not exactly calculated to present Johnson in a favorable
light: "Ex-State G.O.P. Chairman William Johnson of Hanover,
who thus far has based his senatorial primary campaign on an in-
cessant series of attacks against the Loeb newspapers, yesterday
took the extreme step of denying a story before it was published."[13]

From May on, there were almost no well publicized clashes
between Johnson and Loeb; a minor exception occurred late in
June when the candidate challenged the publisher to meet him
in the *Union Leader* offices. Johnson felt that his fight with Loeb
had lost its novelty and news value. He largely confined himself
to a strategy of responding to Loeb attacks rather than initiating
confrontations himself. He reasoned that since Loeb was not a
candidate, it would look a little foolish for a politician to attack
him constantly; and it would also look like a negative approach,
as if the candidate had no positive appeals to make. In retrospect,
Johnson thinks that he might have been wise to have goaded Loeb
into making more attacks on him.[14]

Johnson's anti-Loeb strategy was used as a means of projecting
his main campaign appeal, an image of youth, vigor, and ability.
He also tried to present himself as a moderate Republican, a
comparison with General Thyng being implied: "hoping that he
would become an extremist, I could become the voice of moderation."[15] But Johnson refrained from attacking Thyng personally,
in part to avoid alienating Thyng's supporters if Johnson were to
win the primary.

Thyng's main appeal was that of a war hero whose experience
enabled him to know how to deal with the troubling Southeast

13. "Johnson Still Fretting about 'Poll' Reports," *Sunday News* (May 1,
1966), p. 1.
14. Interview with William R. Johnson, May 1, 1968.
15. Ibid., August 9, 1967.

Asian situation. The General tried to make Vietnam the major
issue and took the position that the war was being prosecuted
ineffectively, with too many restrictions on our use of military
power. Thyng also tried to project sincerity and forcefulness in
his face-to-face contact with the voters. One of the General's
drawbacks was his lack of a smooth public-speaking style, a
disadvantage that became evident when he delivered a series of
speeches on a tour of the state as soon as he retired from the Air
Force. He himself felt that his personality did not fit the require-
ments of an outgoing politician.[16]

Thyng encountered some difficulties in his relationships with
the New Hampshire press, in part because of his support by Loeb.
The General thinks now that most of the other editors were so
anti-Loeb that they wrote unfavorable editorials about him before
they had a chance to meet him and discuss the issues with him.
One specific complaint is that these evening daily editors attached
the label of "conservative" to Thyng simply because he was supported by the *Union Leader*.[17] Commenting particularly on the
news coverage of the campaign, a Thyng aide expresses a similar
opinion:

> Philosophically Harry Thyng was a true moderate Republican;
> his position on the federal government was, I'd say, almost
> diametrically opposed to that of Loeb. . . . I think it's an honest
> statement that Harry's differences with them [the *Union Leader*]
> on domestic issues just didn't receive the play in that paper or
> any paper, for that matter, that they should have. I looked on
> it as a matter of the *Union Leader* not being anxious to empha-
> size its differences with Thyng and of the other papers in the
> state just not wanting to let the people think that this fellow
> was anything but an ultra-conservative Loeb candidate.[18]

One reason Thyng had difficulty differentiating his political
philosophy from Loeb's was the strong emphasis the General
placed on his Vietnam position, which was very close to that of
the *Union Leader* publisher. Also, Thyng was probably wary of

16. Interview with Harrison R. Thyng, August 15, 1967.
17. Ibid.
18. Interview, not for attribution, August 10, 1967.

precipitating a break with Loeb and other conservative Republicans. However, several times the General spelled out domestic policy differences between himself and Loeb. On one occasion the *Union Leader* cited Thyng's support of civil rights legislation and Medicare as evidence that he was not inordinately influenced by the newspaper.[19] Moreover, as the General campaigned, he tried to dissociate himself on an individual basis from certain virulent Loeb editorials. After the strong April 14th front-page editorial, Thyng aides reportedly sent word to Loeb requesting him to cease making vitriolic personal attacks; with few exceptions Loeb did refrain from writing such editorials. Nevertheless, the *Union Leader's* support carried with it certain drawbacks for Thyng, especially with regard to other New Hampshire newspapers.

If Thyng thought that the press treated him unfairly, some editors and reporters felt the same way about Thyng. Several newspapermen say they resented Thyng's alleged unavailability to the non-Loeb press and his practice of often feeding material only to the *Union Leader*.[20] It is claimed that Thyng was non-communicative at a State News Service dinner meeting and left early. The General appeared to be highly suspicious of the non-Loeb press; *Valley News* managing editor Stephen Taylor says: "He came here and was actually fairly antagonistic towards us without having any cause to be at all. . . . He started right out with a chip on his shoulder about the other [non-Loeb] papers."[21] One journalist theorizes that Thyng had been briefed by his brother or *Union Leader* personnel to be extremely wary of the "left wing" New Hampshire press.[22] No matter how it started, mutual distrust between Thyng and the non-Loeb papers marred their relationships.

Besides strong editorial support in the early months of the campaign, the *Union Leader* and *Sunday News* also gave General Thyng favorable news coverage. From the day after William Johnson's announcement of candidacy in April through the end of July, key display pages of the Loeb papers carried almost three times

19. "Thyng's Critics Eat a Little Crow," *Union Leader* (April 16, 1966).
20. E.g., "Campaigning under Wraps," *Monitor* (April 22, 1966).
21. Interview with Stephen Taylor, September 20, 1967.
22. Interview with George W. Wilson of the *Monitor*, September 6, 1967.

as many news stories and photos about Thyng as about Johnson.[23] Moreover, the Thyng articles often had a positive slant. The most controversial content was a pair of captions written beneath two large front-page photographs of former President Dwight D. Eisenhower, in New Hampshire for the Exeter graduation of his grandson, shaking hands with General Thyng. The caption implied (but did not state directly) that Ike supported Thyng's candidacy.[24] Eisenhower later affirmed his position of neutrality in the senatorial primary. In a news story and editorials, though, the *Union Leader* and *Sunday News* suggested that the former President *really* wanted Thyng to win, even if no formal endorsement had been made.[25]

In the closing days of the filing period in late July, Thyng and Johnson were joined by three other major candidates for the Republican senatorial nomination. The new entrants were former Governors Lane Dwinell and Wesley Powell, and Doloris Bridges, widow of the late Senator Styles Bridges. The field was swelled to six contestants including a minor candidate, truck driver and former 1964 Lodge delegate Harold W. Ayer.

On Tuesday, July 26, Lane Dwinell of Lebanon officially entered the Senate race. Dwinell had served two terms in the State House from 1954 through 1958 and had not run for office since. Considered to be a moderate on the New Hampshire political spectrum, Dwinell calculated that he had a good chance of beating Thyng and Johnson. The former Governor felt that he was ideologically closer to most Republican voters than Thyng (on the right) and Johnson (on the left). Moreover, in terms of appeal with the electorate, "I and some people whose judgment I respected thought that neither Thyng nor Johnson was taking hold awfully strongly."[26] Dwinell concedes that these two candidates had built up more strength than he estimated. A poll probably would have changed Dwinell's calculation on this point.

23. These statistics and others in this chapter are based on an examination of newspaper content explained below, Chapter 5 and Appendix C.

24. *Sunday News* (June 12, 1966), and *Union Leader* (June 13, 1966).

25. "Says Ike Backs No Candidates in Primaries," *Union Leader* (July 1, 1966), p. 1. " 'Please Non-Endorse ME, General!' " *Union Leader* (July 2, 1966). "It's News at Last!" *Sunday News* (July 3, 1966).

26. Interview with Lane Dwinell, August 22, 1967.

In retrospect the former Governor thinks that his late entry doomed whatever chances he might have had for the nomination. Dwinell says that friends had urged him to enter earlier in the year. Why hadn't he taken their advice? For one thing, Dwinell had been occupied with a pressing business venture. Also, he had a strong aversion to spending a lot of money, and "You can't spend as much money in seven weeks as you could in seven months." Another personal reason also operated:

> I'll be very frank, and I don't mind being quoted on this: I hate campaigning. I'm not so complacent or naive that l think anybody can get to be a United States Senator without working for it. But to me a political campaign is so damn miserable that even if you have a goal such as the United States Senate, I always do an awful lot of soul searching to find out whether I want to go through all that agony.[27]

July 27, the day after Dwinell's announcement, Mrs. Doloris Bridges dropped a bombshell by entering the race. In late 1965 she had told General Thyng that she intended to support him if he ran, and she had given no indications that she would become a candidate herself. Perhaps the entry of a second moderate in the person of Dwinell caused her to reassess her chances, which would be further improved by the anticipated announcement of Wesley Powell, whose candidacy would further fragment the vote. Moreover, she had run strongly in the 1962 senatorial primary, and she was well known throughout the state. At any rate, Mrs. Bridges discerned critical weaknesses in the other candidates:

> I couldn't somehow see New Hampshire buying the sword-rattling approach, particularly when they had so decidedly discarded such an approach two years before in the presidential primary in the candidacy of Senator Goldwater. I couldn't quite see them adopting the nothingness of Bill Johnson's campaign. I couldn't see them supporting a candidate who had repudiated the Republican Party in former Governor Powell. I couldn't see them supporting a man like Governor Dwinell who hadn't run for public office or even been active making

27. Ibid.

speeches in the state for years. So I considered it seemed rather a wide-open field.[28]

Events were to show, however, that Mrs. Bridges was underestimating the support of the other candidates and overestimating her own strength.

Few politicians were surprised at the July 28th announcement of former Governor Wesley Powell (1958-1962), who had run for major office in each of the previous six election years. Powell, with an ardent following that transcended ideological lines, was a special threat in a multicandidate field. Like Dwinell, both Mrs. Bridges and Powell blame their failure to win in part on their late entry.[29]

The rationality of at least two of the final three decisions to enter the race can be questioned. Johnson is able to make a persuasive argument, based on certain assumptions about the size of the moderate vote, that Dwinell's decision to run made sense only if he thought he could defeat Johnson by approximately 26,000 votes to 2,000.[30] If one adopts Dwinell's structuring of the decision and adds the information he sought and had at his disposal, however, his entry can be logically justified. A similar argument can be made in the case of Mrs. Bridges. Each candidate used a framework and information which weighted the decision in favor of his own entry into the race. The apparently rational calculations may have been more nearly rationalizations of deeper impulses, even before the final decisions to run were reached.

The theme of experience was dominant in the overt public appeals of the three new candidates. Former Governors Dwinell and Powell stressed their experience in high public office. Mrs. Bridges recalled the years she had spent in Washington and emphasized her knowledge of foreign affairs. Like General Thyng, Mrs. Bridges employed Vietnam as her major public issue. The positions of Thyng's opponents were more complex than his all-out, win-the-war approach, but there were no fundamental breaks with the premise of American commitment to South

28. Interview with Doloris Bridges, August 16, 1967.
29. Ibid.; interview with Wesley Powell, July 18, 1967. Governor Powell declined to have his interview quoted directly.
30. Interview with William R. Johnson, August 9. 1967.

Vietnam. Dwinell remarks, "There weren't any doves; we just weren't *experienced* hawks like Thyng."[31]

Johnson's attempt to make William Loeb an issue was continued by Powell, who occasionally spoke of the "Loeb-Thyng combination." (Powell and Loeb had been bitter enemies since late 1961, when the publisher sharply reversed his previous support of the Governor.) Mrs. Bridges and Dwinell did not add to the attack on Loeb; Dwinell recalls, "I said when I was asked about it that I didn't consider that Bill Loeb was an issue."[32]

For its part, the *Union Leader* continued to back Thyng strongly in its editorials but virtually ignored the other candidates. In news coverage the Loeb papers kept up their support of Thyng; from the time all candidates had announced until the end of the primary campaign, key display pages of the *Union Leader* and *Sunday News* carried twice as many news stories and photos of Thyng as of all four of his opponents.

Johnson kept up his determined efforts to cultivate the press and win editorial support. One practice tailored for this purpose was the preparation of weekly position papers, written with the help of campaign assistant David Hess. Johnson recalls:

> We used to laugh; they were being written for twenty-five people, twenty-five editors of newspapers. And out of those twenty-five, only one out of every paper was ever read. But every week from this desk was a nice, thick paper written by us coming in, and they say, "What a thoughtful young man!" This was part of the image that a newspaperman wants to have, he particularly. He's a thoughtful person who can write well, writes cogently, writes quickly, and expresses himself well. That's their trade; they know the management of words, and therefore you must impress them that you know how to write well and can write precisely.[33]

One newspaper whose endorsement Johnson was particularly eager to obtain was the Concord *Monitor*, traditionally considered

31. Interview with Lane Dwinell, August 22, 1967.
32. Ibid.
33. Interview with William R. Johnson, July 31, 1967.

to be the voice of the Republican establishment in New Hampshire. Johnson felt that the *Monitor*'s endorsement would win a few votes but would be more valuable as an aid for garnering the support of other newspapers. The candidate built his relationship with *Monitor* assistant publisher Thomas Gerber and general manager George Wilson, seeing them often and asking their advice on his press relations. Johnson thought that Gerber and Wilson had implicitly indicated that their paper would endorse him. However, former publisher James M. Langley had retained control over endorsements when he had sold the paper several years before. On August 3 the *Monitor* endorsed Lane Dwinell.[34] Johnson was furious at losing the endorsement, though this was the first and last pro-Dwinell editorial to appear in the paper. Johnson felt that Dwinell was a particular threat because of his ideological and geographical proximity to the Hanover candidate; thus Johnson thought that both men were to a great extent competing for the same voters.

A dramatic mistake by Dwinell hurt him and possibly helped Johnson's vote total. An August 17th news story began:

> Former Gov. Lane Dwinell, candidate for the Republican nomination for the U.S. Senate, today disclosed that Federal Judge Howard F. Corcoran, who issued a short-lived order Monday barring the House Committee on Un-American Activities from holding a hearing yesterday on a bill forbidding Americans to aid the Viet Cong, is the brother of Thomas Corcoran, whom Dwinell termed a "notorious lobbyist for wealthy industrialists and financial backer of Sen. Thomas McIntyre."[35]

Though Dwinell says he must take responsibility for the statement, he points out that a staff member inserted the guilt-by-association language linking McIntyre to Judge Corcoran.[36]

Johnson meant to capitalize on the Dwinell slip and wrote a statement decrying the use of guilt by association. Always concerned about press support, he then set out to ensure good news

34. "We'll Go with Dwinell," *Monitor* (August 3, 1966).
35. "Dwinell Links Judge to McIntyre Backer," *Union Leader* (August 17, 1966), p. 1.
36. Interview with Lane Dwinell, August 25, 1967.

coverage and editorial backing for *his* statement which came close
to attacking a fellow candidate:

> I tried to call every single newspaper editor who was friendly
> toward me, and I asked them if I should make the statement.
> . . . And thirteen editors—thank God!—all said, "Oh yes, you
> ought to make the statement." The conscious thing was twofold.
> One, by calling them beforehand and getting them to say, "Yes,
> you ought to make the statement," you know now it's going to
> be on page one, lead position, because the editor has been in on
> the decision as to whether or not you ought to make the state-
> ment. Number two, you know it's going to be followed up by
> an editorial saying what a courageous statement it was or what a
> wise statement it was because the editor himself had been part
> of the decision making as to whether or not you should make
> it. . . . And the story got terrific play, front page everywhere—and
> editorial support. And Lane Dwinell's campaign fell on its face.
> From that moment on he was dead.[37]

Dwinell also reports that his supporters were very discouraged
by the incident and that his campaign suffered a noticeable setback.[38] At the same time, Johnson earned the resentment of
people who felt that he had taken unfair advantage of Dwinell.
However, Johnson feels that he definitely reaped the net benefit
of the controversy.[39]

One of the reactions to Dwinell's statement was a strong Concord
Monitor editorial written by Thomas Gerber which criticized the
Monitor's endorsed candidate for his press release: "It has diluted
his stature as a man of moderation with knowledge of the ways
of public affairs and a sense of justice."[40]

Johnson's determined wooing of the press helped him obtain
many more endorsements than any of his opponents. He used
this endorsement advantage in his late-campaign advertising, which
showed that he was backed by a total of fifteen daily and weekly
papers, compared with four for Powell, two for Thyng, one for

37. Interview with William R. Johnson, August 9, 1967.
38. Interview with Lane Dwinell, August 25, 1967.
39. Interview with William R. Johnson, August 9, 1967.
40. "Be Fair," *Monitor* (August 19, 1966).

Dwinell, and none for Bridges and Ayer. Among the six dailies making endorsements, Johnson received four with one each for Thyng and Dwinell.[41] In retrospect Johnson does not think that losing the *Monitor's* support was a significant blow to him, though he believes that the paper's backing might have made it *easier* for him to obtain the endorsements of other newspapers.[42]

Reviewing the amount of attention he devoted to the press during the campaign, Johnson says: "I think that I spent half of my time trying to woo the media, because I was so convinced I had to have a counterforce to the Loeb people. And I think it was worthwhile; I don't rate that as a mistake. I think it was a very important thing to me."[43]

One other candidate made a notable effort to use the media to his advantage. On several occasions Wesley Powell, known for his spell-binding speaking style on television, bought time on New Hampshire's one VHF commercial TV station. Following a standard practice for him, Powell advertised his TV appearances in front-page ads in several newspapers.

On September 13, New Hampshire Republicans nominated General Thyng for the Senate. The election returns read as follows:[44]

Thyng	22,741	30%
Powell	18,145	24
Johnson	17,410	23
Dwinell	10,781	14
Bridges	7,613	10
Ayer	351	0
	77,041	101%

The unanimous opinion of those interviewed is that *Union Leader* support was a major factor in Thyng's victory, particularly through building up voter recognition of a previously unknown candidate. Nevertheless, several observers feel that some of Loeb's editorials were not helpful for his candidate. In this connection, the inter-

41. Johnson advertisement, *Union Leader* (September 12, 1966), p. 1.
42. Interview with William R. Johnson, May 1, 1968.
43. Ibid., August 9, 1967.
44. Basic source: *State of New Hampshire Manual for the General Court, 1967* (Concord: Department of State), pp. 294-295.

viewees agree that *Union Leader* news coverage was more beneficial to Thyng than its editorials. For example, a member of Thyng's
campaign staff says:

> Let's face it: Harry Thyng got a million dollars' worth of free
> publicity from the *Union Leader*, and I don't think that there is
> any question but that the *Union Leader* helped him during the
> primary. . . . I think that the news coverage during the primary
> and during the election helped Harry Thyng more than anything
> else and that a definite negative factor in the campaign was some
> of Loeb's editorial support of Thyng; I am referring specifically
> to the one that referred to Bill Johnson and all his supporters as
> Ivy League eggheads, leftists, everything.[45]

Concerning Loeb's support, Lane Dwinell suggests: "It's a two-
edged sword, if you will. I think in Thyng's case the net result was
beneficial because he was not known."[46]

The *Union Leader* may have been successful in transmitting a favorable image of Thyng to the voting public; but it should also be
emphasized that the General, a forceful man with a brilliant military record and few political enemies, had attractive characteristics. The Loeb papers did a good job in selling their product, but
they had a good product to sell. In accounting for Thyng's success,
however, one should not overlook the importance of the multicandidate field. The General probably would have had considerable
difficulty beating Johnson, Dwinell, or Powell in a head-to-head
battle. The large number of contestants and the absence of a run-
off primary probably aided Loeb's candidate.

Johnson ran much more strongly than many New Hampshire political veterans had expected. We have seen the importance of the
Union Leader in his strategic calculations. Was the anti-Loeb strategy a factor behind his strength? A number of interviewees think
that attacking the *Union Leader* publisher helped Johnson. Others
disagree, like Mrs. Bridges:

> I think it's sheer insanity to attack newspapers in a campaign.
> It is an old political truism that nobody who has any political

45. Interview, not for attribution, August 10, 1967.
46. Interview with Lane Dwinell, August 25, 1967.

know-how takes on a newspaper. . . . And I thought Bill showed complete naivete when he attacked Loeb. He couldn't possibly win that battle; it was ridiculous. Certainly he gained comfort and support from some of his followers, but those people were going to be for him anyway.[47]

A member of Senator McIntyre's staff reasons:

I'm not sure that strategy was right for Bill Johnson. . . . Had I been Bill Johnson, I would have made some appeal to the same kind of people who were supporting Thyng . . . because he needed that kind of support. The Republican primary is not unlike the Democratic primary in that the bulk of the vote still comes from the readership area of the Manchester *Union Leader*— not as much so as the Democratic primary but a good deal of it. . . . I'm not sure that I would have picked an open fight with Loeb, because solidifying the anti-Loeb Republican support was not enough to get him through a primary. He needed other support. I'm sure that he felt that he could win with anti-Loeb support alone.[48]

Indeed, Johnson felt that he did not need the support of conservative Republican voters and thinks he was wise to attack Loeb.

The Senatorial General Election

William Loeb had been a constant critic of Senator Thomas J. McIntyre since the latter's election in 1962. These attacks intensified in 1965 and continued through the Republican primary. The *Union Leader* was a major factor in the strategic calculations of McIntyre and his advisers. As in the primary, Loeb was to become a topic of discussion in the general election campaign, for McIntyre decided to attack the publisher openly and to accuse General Thyng of being a "Loeb puppet."

The McIntyre camp began its systematic preparations early in 1966. Vietnam and inflation were seen as the probable major is-

47. Interview with Doloris Bridges, August 16, 1967.
48. Interview, not for attribution, September 28, 1967.

sues, and McIntyre's handling of them was anticipated. At the same time, rough strategies were formulated for each of the possible Republican opponents. As the summer progressed, McIntyre held regular strategy sessions with members of his staff and other friends in the Democratic Party. One of these participants recalls: "There were some strategy meetings every week. Tom had a big gang of us. We used to sit at a meeting every Sunday morning at breakfast. And we would all sit around and chew the fat. We would talk over all these things, and this [the selection of a campaign strategy] was a concerted decision."[49]

The participants at these meetings seriously considered adopting an anti-Loeb strategy if Thyng were to win the Republican nomination. A McIntyre staff member reports that the anti-Loeb tactic was considered as a possible strategy against a potential Republican opponent other than Thyng—a candidate whom Loeb would back over the Senator.[50] When McIntyre filed for reelection on July 25, he issued a statement proclaiming that Vietnam would probably be the chief national issue and that "it is certain that the paramount state issue will be the vicious, cancerous Loeb press and its manipulated operations against any candidate that does not choose to buckle under to its dictatorial publisher."[51] McIntyre's statement was run in a page one *Union Leader* story which also included a response by Loeb. Perhaps the Senator hoped for this publicity and wanted to observe the reaction to a trial attack against the publisher.

By primary day a firm decision had been reached among McIntyre and his advisers to use the Loeb-Thyng connection as a major issue, together with strong anti-Loeb statements, if Thyng were to be the opponent. This conclusion was reached despite the feeling of some McIntyre associates that it would be undignified for a United States Senator to embroil himself in a fight with a publisher. Moreover, it was felt that a newspaper had the advantage of being able to have the last word in a debate with a candidate. One aide says that McIntyre anticipated the amount of abuse

49. Interview with Joseph A. Millimet, August 28, 1967.

50. Interview, not for attribution, September 28, 1967.

51. "McIntyre, Loeb Trade Comment on N.H. Issues," *Union Leader* (July 26, 1966), p. 1.

he would have to take from the *Union Leader*: "He had to campaign on the issue of Loeb, and it's personally not very satisfying to have to do it."[52]

Nevertheless, the anti-Loeb strategy was selected. A prime consideration was that if McIntyre were to attack Loeb, he would lose little in addition to his already unfavorable news and editorial treatment by the *Union Leader*. Second, one of Thyng's great liabilities appeared to be the perception among voters of his connection with Loeb. It was thought that many people had first heard of the General through the *Union Leader* and had no distinct image of him separate from the newspaper and its controversial publisher. A McIntyre adviser says: "After all, Thyng was a real American hero; and you can't attack somebody like that unless you have a sure plan to do it, and we did."[53] Furthermore a campaign against Loeb would be an extension of a theme sounded by William Johnson and Wesley Powell in the Republican primary. It was felt that McIntyre would thus receive the sympathy and support of many Republicans who opposed Thyng's nomination. Another factor in the McIntyre calculations was the anticipated generous news coverage and editorial support from the non-Loeb press. In this connection, the perceived success of Johnson was considered. A member of McIntyre's inner circle of advisers recalls: "Johnson did very well in the Republican primary—much better than anybody thought he was going to do, except Johnson. He did very, very well. Everybody was astounded at how well he did in the primary. And a lot of people, including ourselves, thought that some of this was due to his willingness to fight Loeb."[54] A member of the Senator's staff observes: " So our choice was rather simple, I suppose. You either fight him or you don't. And we felt that there was political advantage in fighting him."[55]

The anti-Loeb strategy was carried much further by McIntyre than by Johnson, who used it only in the early stages of his campaign. By contrast, McIntyre made the attack on Loeb and his

52. Interview with John Barker, September 25, 1967.
53. Interview, not for attribution, July 20, 1967.
54. Interview with Joseph A. Millimet, August 28, 1967.
55. Interview, not for attribution, September 28, 1967.

connection with Thyng the main issue in the Senator's campaign.

Positively, the McIntyre strategy was to project an impression of the Senator as being moderate, independent, and responsible. By contrast Thyng would be pictured as an immoderate extremist, a candidate hand-picked by and controlled by William Loeb, and too irresponsible to make important national decisions.

McIntyre wasted little time in blasting Loeb. Three days after the primary, the Senator issued a statement calling Loeb's activities "a cancerous growth on the progress of our State." The Senator proclaimed:

> I see no need to expose William Loeb and the Manchester *Union Leader*, because the bulk of the responsible people of this state are entirely aware of Loeb's attempts to take control of the Republican Party and use Harrison R. Thyng as his personal voice in the United States Senate . . . anyone who reads the Manchester *Union Leader* is entirely aware that Harrison Thyng is nothing more than a parrot for the Loeb press. . . .
>
> In last Tuesday's Primary, a small minority of the Republican Party was able to nominate a newspaper instead of a candidate for a seat in the United States Senate. The effort to nominate my opponents—Loeb and Thyng—was financed, supported and encouraged by the Goldwater wing of the party. . . .
>
> As your United States Senator I appeal to the conscience of the state's responsible press and to Republicans, Democrats, and Independents alike, to join with me and the fair-minded people of this state to thwart this power move by a single newspaper and its puppet candidate—financed and encouraged by the forces of extremism that this nation can well do without.[56]

Loeb responded several days later as he criticized the "vicious blast at this newspaper and its publisher last Friday." Claiming that McIntyre was trying to sidetrack the *Union Leader's* exposure of the Senator's record, Loeb commented, "This is an old technique, developed to a fine art by the Nazis and the Communists,"[57]

56. Reprint of "McIntyre Raps Thyng," Portsmouth *Herald* article (September 16, 1966). Obtained from Senator McIntyre's office.

57. "There Is Nothing So Powerful as Truth," *Union Leader* (September 20, 1966), p. 1.

Two members of McIntyre's staff say that they were very satisfied with the news coverage of and editorial reaction to the Senator's attack on Loeb. One of these assistants indicates that the
response of the non-Loeb press came as no surprise:

Q. This may be hard to recall exactly, but did the degree of the
reaction surprise you at the time? Had you been expecting it?
A. We expected it. Simply because at any time the *Union Leader*
takes a strong position on anything—I don't care what it is—
many of the other daily newspapers in the state will immediately
take the other side.[58]

General Thyng strongly resented the charge that he was a puppet
of William Loeb. Thyng asserted it was Loeb's right to endorse
whomever he wished but that the publisher exerted no control
over the General. In the interview Thyng stated that it was ridiculous to claim that anyone with his military laurels could be controlled by a newspaper publisher.[59]

On Vietnam, Thyng's major issue, McIntyre by and large supported Administration policy. But rather than simply defend that
policy against Thyng's charges, McIntyre acted to put the General
on the defensive. In an April speech quoted by the Concord
Monitor, Thyng had asserted that he could end the war in ten days
if given the chance. McIntyre repeated that statement and asked
whether Thyng was advocating the use of nuclear weapons, an im-
plication which Thyng hotly denied.

For McIntyre, though, the big issue was Loeb and his connection
with Thyng. The Senator constantly attacked the publisher and
branded Thyng a "Loeb puppet." Then in early October McIntyre
challenged the inarticulate Thyng to a public debate. The General
did not accept the challenge, but Loeb dramatically injected himself into the debate picture in a bizarre turn of events. To the as-
tonishment of political observers, across the top of the front page
of the October 16 *Sunday News* appeared a debate challenge from
Loeb to McIntyre. The publisher's telegram to McIntyre read, in
part:

58. Interview, not for attribution, September 28, 1967.
59. Interview with Harrison R. Thyng, August 15, 1967.

In almost daily utterances and press releases you proclaim that
Loeb and the Loeb papers are the real issue, the only issue in
this campaign.

Obviously I am not a candidate, nor an issue, in anything.

But since you insist that I am I have decided to challenge—and
hereby do challenge—you to a television debate on the McIntyre
record in Washington. . . .[60]

Apparently Loeb felt that he could embarrass McIntyre in a public encounter. However, the Senator pounced upon the Loeb challenge as an illustration of his "puppet" charges: "Two weeks ago I
challenged Harrison Thyng to join me in public debate of the issues
in this campaign, and I am astonished to find Mr. Loeb responding
for him. I feel it is enlightening to the voters of our state that Harrison Thyng would permit William Loeb to function as his stand
in"[61] McIntyre accepted Loeb's challenge to debate on the condition that General Thyng attend also. Thyng naturally wanted no
part of this arrangement. Loeb renewed his challenge to debate
McIntyre face to face, but to no avail. The publisher eventually
bought television time himself to answer McIntyre but had to
switch to other subjects in his October 31 talk when it was pointed
out that the expense would have to be charged to the Thyng campaign financial statement.

The evening daily papers (as well as the *Union Leader*) gave the
debate controversy generous play. The moderate press also casti-
gated Loeb in editorials. For example, the Concord *Monitor* lik-
ened Loeb and Thyng to Edgar Bergen and Charlie McCarthy.[62]
Later the *Monitor* commented on the debate incident and Loeb's
scheduled television appearance: "This development has been a
perfect example of how Loeb takes over and dominates the candi-

60. "Loeb Challenges McIntyre to Debate," *Sunday News* (October 16,
1966), p. 1.

61. From "McIntyre Dodges TV Bid," *Union Leader* (October 19, 1966),
p. 1.

62. "Campaign Flak," *Monitor* (October 18, 1966).

At least one moderate evening daily newspaper asserted that the "Loeb
puppet" charge was inaccurate and unfair to Thyng—Keene *Sentinel* editorial
reprinted in the *Union Leader* (October 26, 1966). The *Sentinel* endorsed
McIntyre.

dacies of those he supports. If Thyng thought he could have Loeb's
support and escape such a predicament he was naive about the
political facts of life in New Hampshire in recent years. It is possible that the General might benefit from a backlash of sympathy
if Loeb persists in his egotistical binge."[63]

McIntyre received the editorial endorsements of four dailies, an
unusually strong showing for a Democrat. Three papers supported
Thyng and two made no formal endorsements."[64] By contrast,
McIntyre's running mate, Governor John King, received the backing of no daily newspapers.

As the McIntyre strategists had anticipated, the *Union Leader*
and *Sunday News* gave the Senator much less generous coverage
than General Thyng. From the close of the primary until election
day, the Loeb papers printed thirty-four news stories about Thyng
and nineteen about McIntyre in key display pages; these stories
include only those whose headlines were not obviously unfavorable to the candidate. In addition, seventeen overtly unfavorable
stories about McIntyre appeared, compared with one about Thyng.
Twenty-seven photographs of Thyng were printed during the campaign, eight of McIntyre. Finally, fifty-eight editorials on the Senate race were carried in the *Union Leader* and *Sunday News*; I
classify fourteen as being pro-Thyng, thirty-five as anti-McIntyre,
and nine as both pro-Thyng and anti-McIntyre.

Thus the Loeb press changed its strategy from the primary campaign pattern of praising Thyng and ignoring his opponents in editorials. The general election advocacy of the two papers was
predominantly anti-McIntyre—not only in editorials but also in
news articles. The dominant theme in the anti-McIntyre attacks
was that the Senator was nothing more than a "rubber stamp" for
the Johnson Administration's foreign and domestic politics, which
the *Union Leader* claimed were disastrous for the nation.

The campaign's final two weeks saw the McIntyre forces intro-

63. "Courting a Backlash," *Monitor* (October 25, 1966).

64. Supporting McIntyre were the Claremont *Eagle*, Keene *Sentinel*, Lebanon *Valley News*, and Portsmouth *Herald*. Thyng won the endorsements of
the Manchester *Union Leader*, Nashua *Telegraph*, and Dover *Democrat*. The
Concord *Monitor* and the Laconia *Citizen* endorsed neither candidate. "Editors' Choices Favor Republicans, McIntyre," *Monitor* (November 7, 1966), p. 1.

duce a new technique: attacking William Loeb in advertisements placed on the front page of the *Union Leader*. This tactic was adopted in large part because of dissatisfaction with *Union Leader* news coverage. Speaking about Manchester, a McIntyre adviser states, "If we had had to rely on news stories, I'm afraid we never could have got our message through in that area at all."[65] Mc-Intyre bought five ads flailing Loeb and tying Thyng to the *Union Leader* publisher; three of the ads ran on consecutive days during the final weekend of the campaign. A sampling of the McIntyre displays finds one ad which begins, "Senator Tom McIntyre Challenges General Harrison Thyng to Cut Himself Free of William Loeb's Puppet Strings." Underneath are listed several colorfully critical Loeb quotes about various political figures (President Eisenhower—"that stinking hypocrite," "Dopey Dwight"; Senator Margaret Chase Smith—"Moscow Maggie"). Next comes a quote from Thyng saying he was delighted to have *Union Leader* support. The ad continues, "Now is the time to speak out, General . . . Are you—or are you not—A Willing Puppet of William Loeb??"[66] Another McIntyre front-page *Union Leader* ad implores voters to "Beware the Loeb/Thyng Combination—Vote Independent—Vote Moderate—Re-Elect U.S. Senator McIntyre."[67] Interviewees expressing an opinion on these advertisements all believe that they were a clever and helpful device for McIntyre.

Senator McIntyre won the November 8 election with 54 percent of the vote, or an 18,500-vote margin over General Thyng.[68] Although the *Leader*-backed candidate failed to win the general election, several interviewees credit the paper with influencing the outcome of that contest. The reasoning is that by helping to nominate a weak candidate in the Republican primary, Loeb made it easier for McIntyre to win the general election. And like the primary, it is felt by a number of observers that some of Loeb's efforts to help Thyng lost rather than won votes for the General. The publisher's challenge to debate McIntyre is thought to have been especially harmful to Thyng.

65. Interview, not for attribution, September 28, 1967.

66. McIntyre advertisement, *Union Leader* (October 29, 1966), p. 1.

67. McIntyre advertisement, *Union Leader* (November 7, 1966), p. 1.

68. Basic source: *State of New Hampshire Manual for the General Court, 1967* (Concord: Department of State), p. 438.

Although the interviewees are split on the success of Johnson's anti-Loeb strategy, they generally agree that McIntyre's anti-Loeb tactics were helpful (of course Johnson lost and McIntyre won). The Senator's anti-Loeb, front-page *Union Leader* ads are the most highly praised single maneuver by McIntyre. Asked for proof of the impact of these ads, a McIntyre staff member replies that voters specifically discussed these anti-Loeb blasts while the Senator was campaigning in Manchester.[69] Another McIntyre adviser states that although McIntyre ran poorly in Manchester, his page one ads kept him from doing even less well in that city[70] (this assertion is impossible to prove or disprove through examination of available voting and survey data). A Thyng aide agrees that the attempt to tie the General to Loeb hurt Thyng: "I also think that Loeb was an issue in the campaign; and while I wouldn't go to the extent of saying that it was a deciding issue, I think that certainly a substantial percentage of the margin of loss was attributable to the anti-Loeb feeling. We were always bucking this Loeb puppet idea; we were on the defensive about it."[71]

This statement warns us against simplisticly attributing the outcome of the election to the *Union Leader*. Obviously, other factors were important as well. For example, McIntyre may have succeeded in conveying a personal image of ability and moderation, and Thyng may be correct that his personality did not help him with the voters. The Loeb press was a significant factor in this election—but only in addition to and in combination with other influences.

69. Interview, not for attribution, September 28, 1967.
70. Interview with Joseph A. Millimet, August 28, 1967.
71. Interview, not for attribution, August 10, 1967.

CHAPTER THREE

A Broader Look at the Strategic Impact

We have seen that, directly or indirectly, the expectation of *Union Leader* support had much to do with General Thyng's decision to retire from the Air Force and run for the Senate. Several of those interviewed stated that another 1966 Republican candidate, James J. Barry, probably would not have run had he not received a clear indication that he would be backed by the Loeb press. Barry, reportedly a close friend of *Union Leader* Editorial Page Editor James Finnegan, denies, however, that his entry decision was crucially influenced by anticipation of the paper's support.[1] Indeed, Barry had been viewed for some time as a potential gubernatorial candidate; as State Commissioner of Health and Welfare he had been embroiled in numerous controversies with Democratic Governor John W. King. It would be implausible to argue that the *Union Leader* recruited Barry into electoral politics, and it is impossible to know precisely how important the anticipation of Loeb backing was for Barry's decision to run in 1966.

Similarly ambiguous conclusions must be made in assessing the possible influence of the Loeb press on the entry decisions of two more recent candidates supported by the *Union Leader.* In 1968 Meldrim Thomson, Jr.—a politically unknown law-book publisher whose most recent venture into electoral politics had been to lose a local school board election—was narrowly defeated by two other candidates in the Republican gubernatorial primary. After another close loss in 1970, Thomson was elected governor in 1972. On the

1. Interview with James J. Barry, November 3, 1967.

Democratic side, retired Navy Captain and former State Commissioner of Economic Development Roger J. Crowley, Jr., won his party's gubernatorial primaries in 1970 and 1972 but lost both general elections. A friend of *Union Leader–Sunday News* Editor-in-Chief B. J. McQuaid,[2] Crowley, like Thomson, obviously harbored political ambitions.

It is possible that the Loeb press did not influence the entry decisions of Barry, Thomson, and Crowley. It is safe to say, however, that these men would not have been *viable* candidates without *Union Leader* backing—at least in their first race, before they had become known to a substantial proportion of the electorate.

At the congressional level, 1962 presents a more clear-cut case. Loeb encouraged a man to run who might not have been a candidate in the absence of the publisher's urging. In the process Loeb may have indirectly played a major role in determining who would represent New Hampshire's Second Congressional District for more than a decade. Ironically, *Union Leader* circulation is much lower in the Second District (which has five daily newspapers of its own) than in the First District. Furthermore, the victor was a liberal Republican who had been bitterly opposed by Loeb.

The Second District opening resulted when Congressman Perkins Bass decided to run for the Senate seat vacated by the 1961 death of Styles Bridges. The major contenders for the Republican nomination were thought to be Bert F. Teague, who appealed to the more conservative elements, and moderate-liberal James C. Cleveland. Teague announced his candidacy on January 24, Cleveland on February 9.

Teague reports that soon after his announcement he paid a visit to Loeb. The candidate argued that the publisher should support him as the only Republican with a chance to defeat Cleveland, a state senator who had drawn strong attacks from Loeb (Teague says Loeb told him that Cleveland's election would be a "disaster").[3] However, Loeb had formed a dislike for Teague, who

2. In 1972 Crowley stated, "I have known B. J. McQuaid for many years. We are close personal friends." "Crowley Charges Blackout by Some Papers in State," *Union Leader* (October 3, 1972), p. 1. In that year's general election the *Union Leader* endorsed Thomson over Crowley.

3. Interview with Bert F. Teague, July 27, 1967.

had been a close associate of former Governor Hugh Gregg, an old enemy of the *Union Leader* publisher.

Loeb had another candidate in mind, New Hampshire Farm Bureau head Stacey W. Cole. Loeb states:

> This is one of the best fellows I've seen come along in New Hampshire politics in many years. He's a very homely sort of fellow and a real backwoods farmer type, but when he gets on a platform he can out-talk Norris Cotton—a very brilliant fellow, very brilliant organizer. And I felt that he would make an ideal congressman. So I preferred to lose with Stacey than going for either of the other two. I think Teague is supposed to be conservative, but I have never had much confidence in Teague. And Cleveland, I feel the same way.[4]

Teague recalls: "The thing that killed me the most was that Mr. Loeb took it upon himself to get Stacey Cole in the race; and this is no secret. . . . Stacey is a very fine gentleman. He'd never been in politics before, and he had no desire to get into this one. He told me three days before he filed that this was Loeb's idea, not his."[5] Teague reasoned that Cole appealed to the same people Teague attracted and that almost all Cole's votes would have gone to Teague, not Cleveland.

Cole announced on February 21. After a long campaign that witnessed the entry of three other candidates, the vote totals of the top three finishers were Cleveland, 14,640; Teague, 13,900; and Cole, 6,100.[6] Cleveland went on to win in November and was reelected in 1964, 1966, 1968, 1970, and 1972. Teague states, "Jim Cleveland should thank Bill Loeb more than anyone else in the state of New Hampshire for getting him elected to Congress."[7] Loeb recalls, "Mrs. Teague wrote me a letter afterwards accusing me of ruining her husband's career."[8] It is plausible that by encouraging Cole to run, Loeb helped to influence the outcome of

4. Interview with William Loeb, October 23, 1967.

5. Interview with Bert F. Teague, July 27, 1967.

6. *State of New Hampshire Manual for the General Court, 1963* (Concord: Department of State), p. 285.

7. Interview with Bert F. Teague, July 27, 1967.

8. Interview with William Loeb, October 23, 1967.

the election—even if the *Union Leader* had no impact on the voters. As for Cole, 1962 was his last venture into the electoral arena.

So far we have been concerned with "positive recruitment": the possibility that the anticipation of likely *Union Leader* actions has induced potential candidates to run who otherwise might not have run. There is also "negative recruitment": the discouragement of potential candidates who otherwise might have run.

The first category in the negative recruitment group includes individuals (mainly conservatives) who feel that the support of the *Union Leader* is vital for their success as a candidate; discovering that this desired support is not forthcoming, the person decides not to run. The second category comprises politicians (mainly liberals or moderates) whose political positions are so opposed to the editorial stands of the *Leader* that they do not expect or even hope to win the paper's backing. However, the difference between the *Leader's* relative neutrality and its opposition spells the difference between such a person's running and not running. Anticipating that the Loeb press will actively oppose him, the potential candidate decides not to make the race.

The detection of cases in these two negative recruitment categories is difficult. Indeed, it is hard even to identify the decisions we are trying to explain, since they were made by noncandidates who are themselves difficult to identify. Nevertheless, the interviews offer several clues.

One interviewee advances a specific instance of a potential candidate who considered running for high office but did not because he felt that he needed Loeb's support and discovered that he would not get it. The politician in question is Republican Louis C. Wyman, who had narrowly lost his House of Representatives seat in the 1964 LBJ landslide. A prominent conservative, Wyman evidently wanted to run for the Senate in 1966 and normally might have been expected to attract Loeb's support. But this time Loeb had already chosen his candidate, General Thyng. The person interviewed was then-Republican State Chairman William R. Johnson, who recalls a late 1965 or early 1966 meeting with Wyman:

A. During that conversation with Lou I said, "Lou, why don't you run for the Senate?" He said, "Well, I can't." He reached into his desk and gave me a copy of a letter from Bill Loeb. It was a two-page letter, and the essence of the letter was "You're a nice young man, and you have a great future in politics in New Hampshire. But you're not quite ready yet to be a U.S. Senator, and I think that you ought to return to Congress. I have a candidate in mind for the U.S. Senate. But keep your cool because you're a young man," and so forth.

Q. So Wyman really took this seriously?

A. As far as he was concerned, this was the death warrant. I mean, if he'd been told that he wasn't old enough to be a U.S. Senator it would have had the same effect upon him. The letter from Bill Loeb meant he couldn't run.

Q. Do you think he might have felt rationally that if he didn't have Loeb's support he couldn't make a good race?

A. Yes, I think it was that. . . . He had to play it safe, and the safe way was to have Loeb's support. . . . He shook his head; he had that look on his face of, you know, being resigned to it.

Q. He didn't question it?

A. He didn't question it. There it was; there it was.[9]

Wyman ran for Congress in 1966 and recaptured his seat by a solid margin.

A similar incident involving Congressman Wyman occurred prior to Senator McIntyre's 1972 reelection bid. Early in 1971 Wyman was seriously considering running for the Republican nomination to oppose McIntyre. An interviewee reports, however, that Loeb made an evening speech in which he announced his intention of supporting former Governor Wesley Powell for the Senate seat. The man recalls meeting Wyman the morning after Loeb's speech: "Wyman . . . turned to me and said, 'Did you hear what Bill Loeb did to me last night?'—as if I should console him or something. . . . He was just blitzed by the whole thing."[10] Loeb also trumpeted his message in a front-page editorial titled "Wyman Vs. Powell": "This newspaper sincerely hopes that former Governor Powell will run for the Republican nomination—and certainly we

9. Interview with William R. Johnson, July 31, 1967.
10. Interview, not for attribution, 1972.

intend to support him if he does."[11] Wyman did not run for the
Senate in 1972—Powell ran, with Loeb's fervent support, and won
the primary but lost the general election against McIntyre.[12]

No other similar instances of Loeb's directly discouraging politicians from running were reported in the interviews.

We turn next to potential candidates who would never expect to
receive *Union Leader* endorsement but who might be discouraged
from running through anticipation of Loeb editorial opposition.
Almost all interviewees who were asked stated that some New
Hampshire citizens have considered running and might have become candidates except that they did not want to experience
Loeb's blistering editorial attacks. It is difficult to know how to
assess these replies: how much were they based on hearsay and
how much on specific knowledge of individual decisions? The
name of one moderate Republican was mentioned a handful of
times; but perhaps some observers tended to generalize from one
case to cover others.

Among those attributing significance to the dislike of receiving
Union Leader personal attacks is former State News Service reporter Frank B. Merrick: "When a man decides to run for public
office in New Hampshire, particularly a statewide office, it's not
just a question of [inaudible] as it is in other states. He's also got
to decide whether he wants to take the *Union Leader*'s vilification.
. . . And there have been candidates that have refused to do it."[13]
Former Democratic National Committeeman William L. Dunfey
agrees with this view:

Q. Have there been cases where people might possibly have
run and maybe considered running but did not because they
didn't want to get involved with the newspaper?

11. "Wyman Vs. Powell," editorial, *Union Leader* (February 18, 1971),
p. 1.

12. In an odd sense Loeb might have influenced Powell *not* to run for governor in 1970. According to a widespread rumor, Loeb and Powell made a
"deal" whereby Powell did not run but rather joined Loeb in supporting
Meldrim Thomson, Jr.; in return, Loeb would endorse Powell for the Senate
in 1972. Loeb denies that such a "deal" was actually made (interview with
William Loeb, March 2, 1973), but events unfolded as *if* such an arrangement
had been made.

13. Interview with Frank B. Merrick, May 2, 1968.

A. Yes. I think in the sense that the *Union Leader* puts the heat to you pretty fast. It's a hot prospect. And those who don't take the heat get out fast; or those who realize that the heat might get put on them don't even get in.[14]

Speaking five years after these two statements were recorded, 1972 Democratic gubernatorial candidate Robert E. Raiche agrees strongly that dislike of personal attack is important in keeping certain potential candidates from running:

It prevents good, qualified candidates from running who have a fear of being attacked personally rather than politically. Not just attacked politically, which one who serves in public office expects, but being attacked unfairly and personally. As an example, Mr. Loeb called me a Vietnik; and to myself and most people who are politically sophisticated, that kind of accusation is obviously ridiculous. However, to people who are apolitical, it presents a connotation that Bob Raiche is a commie. It is my belief that this is one of the reasons why people shy away from politics in this state.[15]

However significant the dislike of personal attack may be, it has not prevented some candidates like Raiche from running. A similar example is Senator McIntyre. Speaking one year after McIntyre's 1966 victory over General Thyng, a member of the Senator's staff says that a factor weighing against the decision to attack Loeb as a major part of the strategy was the anticipation of the extra abuse the Senator would have to withstand.[16] Another McIntyre aide reports:

I'm sure if Senator McIntyre were here he would tell you that it's not an easy thing to take. Because Loeb can get quite personal; you never know what he is going to hit you with next. It's extremely difficult for the candidate and I think even more so for his family. And this was a subject that we talked about frequently during the campaign because it bothered the Senator's wife and his daughter. It bothered those of us who were

14. Interview with William L. Dunfey, September 12, 1967.
15. Interview with Robert E. Raiche, October 13, 1972.
16. Interview with John Barker, September 25, 1967.

close to the Senator; and I don't think you can go through a
campaign like that without really living with this thing twenty-
four hours a day. No one enjoys being editorialized against day
in, day out—all kinds of slams, many of which have nothing whatever to do with the campaign.[17]

Nevertheless, the anti-Loeb strategy was selected by McIntyre and
was followed throughout the campaign.

William Loeb himself doubts that his strong personal attacks influence potential candidates not to run.[18] Also skeptical is Dartmouth Government Professor Laurence I. Radway, who cites one
specific case: "Harry Spanos is by our standards here in New
Hampshire a relatively liberal man. I've heard him very often discussing the question of whether to run—very often—we've talked
about it in great detail. He knows damn well the *Union Leader*
would be against him. But that has never been a major point in his
conversations with me; rather, they've been things like family,
money, job, career, this kind of stuff."[19]

The above evidence, though sketchy and suggestive, makes it appear that the *Union Leader* exerts influence by way of both positive and negative recruitment. Just *how much* of this kind of
impact actually takes place is hard to assess.

Candidates' Handling of Issues

Does the Loeb press help determine positions on issues, and does
it induce the candidates to emphasize some issues rather than others? Many interviewees (and especially newspapermen) assert that
the *Union Leader* is a powerful influence on the formulation of
campaign strategies with respect to issues. For example, Concord
Monitor political editor and reporter Rod Paul states: "[The *Union
Leader*] has an immense impact on the way candidates handle issues. I've never known a candidate—for high public office, certainly—who didn't measure down to the last crossing of the "t" and

17. Interview, not for attribution, September 28, 1967.
18. Interview with William Loeb, October 23, 1967.
19. Interview with Laurence I. Radway, August 11, 1972. In late 1973
Spanos announced his candidacy for the governorship.

dotting of the "i" in his own mind where all this fit into how the *Union Leader* would treat it or react to it or deal with it."[20]

On the other hand, a number of politicians deny that the Loeb press has influenced *their* positions on issues. Nineteen seventy-two Democratic gubernatorial candidate Robert E. Raiche is illustrative:

> There are many factors and variables that one must take into consideration when he is getting ready to run a campaign. One of the factors that we gave serious consideration to is the effect of the *Union Leader*. And so in answer to your question, we did give them special treatment, because we gave them extra consideration as to the types of things they would do against me during the campaign. But the newspaper or the special consideration did not in any way change or modify my positions during the campaign.[21]

Whatever specific influence the *Union Leader* may have on candidates' issue positions, the interviews strongly suggest that politicians always take the newspaper into account when formulating their campaign strategies.

The following exchange with a top Democratic adviser supports the hypothesis that the *Union Leader* has general strategic influence but also illustrates the difficulty of obtaining specific evidence of the paper's impact on candidates' issue positions:

> Q. Do you think that, in general, in recent elections candidates have done things differently because of Loeb than they would have done otherwise? In other words, do you think Loeb has had an actual effect on campaign strategies of candidates?
>
> A. Unquestionably.
>
> Q. Could you elaborate just a little bit? [Pause] I suppose, for one thing, the gubernatorial sales tax business may be one example, where a candidate isn't likely to come out in favor of the sales tax openly, partly because of the *Union Leader*.
>
> A. Well, I could go on at length with some concrete examples, but then I'd be talking about other people's campaigns and I'd rather not, really.

20. Interview with Rod Paul, August 25, 1972.
21. Interview with Robert E. Raiche, October 13, 1972.

Q. But this kind of thing—there are stands on issues, things like this that do get influenced?

A. Absolutely. You take a good, hard look at any major political campaign in the state of New Hampshire over the past ten or fifteen years, and you will find that the strategy of each one of those campaigns was designed very much with Mr. Loeb in mind. . . . Without any doubt whatever he is a major factor in any statewide election or district election in the state.[22]

One method of searching for more concrete evidence is to examine the positions emphasized most strongly by the *Union Leader*. If we can detect Loeb impact on candidates' issue positions, we would expect to find such influence in the area of the *Union Leader*'s gut issues. It has in fact, taken vigorous, clear-cut positions on several state issues in gubernatorial campaigns. By far the most salient issue has been Loeb's opposition to new taxes. The *Union Leader* has not been content with candidates' expressed opposition to new levies; in addition, the gubernatorial aspirant must *pledge to veto* a general sales or income tax (which have never existed in New Hampshire) if elected and if such a measure passes the legislature. The *Union Leader* frequently proclaims that the tax issue is important for deciding gubernatorial campaigns. For example, a 1968 editorial refers to the tax veto pledge as "the question which traditionally has decided gubernatorial elections in New Hampshire."[23]

To a lesser degree, certain other policy positions were strongly pushed by the Loeb papers at various times in the 1960's, including advocacy of the sweepstakes, support for the abolition of state price controls on milk, and the adoption of a law to ban the appearance of communist speakers on state college campuses.

An examination of the record shows that from 1960 to 1972 the *Union Leader* made nine endorsements in gubernatorial primaries and six in general elections.[24] All fifteen went to candidates who

22. Interview, not for attribution, September 28, 1967.

23. "The Yes-No-Maybe Candidate," *Union Leader* (May 23, 1968), p. 1.

24. The endorsed candidates in Republican primaries were Wesley Powell (1960), John Pillsbury (1962 and 1964), James J. Barry (1966), and Meldrim Thomson, Jr. (1968, 1970, 1972). The Democratic primary endorsements were for Roger J. Crowley, Jr. (1970, 1972). General election endorsements

pledged that they would veto a broad-base tax if elected. It appears that giving the veto promise is a necessary condition for receiving the *Union Leader's* gubernatorial endorsement.

The veto pledge, though, has not been quite sufficient to obtain Loeb's blessing. In the 1966 general election Democratic candidate John W. King promised to veto new taxes while Republican Hugh Gregg refused to make the pledge, but the *Union Leader* adopted a neutral posture in the race.[25] And in the 1968 Democratic gubernatorial primary more than one candidate pledged to veto while others rejected the pledge, but the Loeb press made no endorsement.

It is difficult to detect concrete cases in which a candidate has taken the veto pledge because of the *Union Leader* rather than other reasons; perhaps the politician would have taken this stand anyway, in the absence of the paper's advocacy. One clue may be a shift in position by a candidate from a stand he had taken prior to the campaign. In fact, John Pillsbury had voted in favor of a sales tax as a member of the legislature but pledged to veto such a levy when he ran for governor with Loeb support in 1962 and 1964. And in 1968 Portsmouth *Herald* and Concord *Monitor* editorials claimed that Loeb-endorsed Meldrim Thomson had publicly supported additional taxation at the 1964 Constitutional Convention.[26] Nineteen sixty-eight candidate Thomson, however, promised to veto any new broad-base tax and to repeal a limited sales tax on rooms and meals. Of course, even if such reports of switches of position are accurate, the candidates involved may have changed their minds for reasons other than the desire to obtain *Union Leader* endorsement.

Former Democratic Governor John W. King provides a fascinating case of possible Loeb influence on issue positions. In a 1967

---

went to Powell (1960), Pillsbury (1962, 1964), Democratic nominee Emile R. Bussiere (1968), Crowley (1970), and Thomson (1972).

25. In his interview (July 24, 1967) Republican Gregg states he has little doubt that the *Union Leader* would have actively opposed him in the general election if he had not been running on the same ticket as General Thyng. This view certainly is plausible.

26. The two editorials came to my attention when they were reprinted in the Lebanon *Valley News* (August 3, and August 28, 1968).

interview a top King aide presumably reflected the Governor's view of the *Union Leader*: "The Manchester *Union Leader* is a major factor in New Hampshire politics. No other newspaper, or radio station, or anything else comes anywhere close to being as important as the *Union Leader*. I don't think anybody runs for state-wide office without one eye on what Bill Loeb is going to do or what he's going to say; and they do this in a positive or a negative way. And they try to avoid getting him attacking you. This has been the Governor's general strategy, to try to stay out of his way."[27]

With a firm political base in his home city of Manchester, King reportedly felt that support of the Manchester paper was not necessary for his political success, but the Governor nevertheless wanted to avoid strong *Union Leader* condemnation. Though he occasionally took positions at odds with Loeb, in his gubernatorial campaigns, King aligned himself with the *Union Leader* on the paper's gut issues: pledge to veto the sales tax, support of the sweepstakes, opposition to milk price controls, and advocacy of a bill that would have banned communist speakers from state colleges.

For its part the *Union Leader*, though it opposed King to a moderate degree when he first ran in 1962, shifted in 1964 and 1966. Loeb indirectly endorsed Republican John Pillsbury in 1964 and remained neutral with regard to King and Hugh Gregg in 1966. It is likely that the *Union Leader* would have endorsed King in these two campaigns if the paper had not been strongly supporting a Republican in other races each year—Barry Goldwater in 1964 and Harrison Thyng in 1966. Perhaps Loeb refrained from backing King because of a belief that endorsing the head of the Democratic state ticket would harm the chances of Loeb-backed Republicans. Although he urged New Hampshire citizens to vote Republican, Loeb had these kind words for King in 1964: "This newspaper makes no secret of the fact that it likes Governor John King personally as an individual, as well as his attitude on the Sweepstakes, his opposition to retail milk control, and to Communists speaking at the University of New Hampshire."[28]

This conciliatory pattern changed in mid-1968, however, when

27. Interview, not for attribution, September 6, 1967.
28. "Issues, Not Personalities," *Union Leader* (September 23, 1964), p. 1.

King announced that he would run for the Senate against incumbent and *Union Leader* favorite Norris Cotton. With no hope of keeping Loeb neutral, King began to take such flagrantly anti-*Union Leader* positions as favoring gun control laws and voicing reservations about the Vietnam war. Loeb was quick to note King's change of direction, as in a June 15 editorial titled "Turncoat King": "As most of our readers know, this newspaper has never been hostile to Gov. King. We have frequently praised many excellent things he has done. Our personal relations with him have been friendly. Therefore, it is with great regret that we notice Gov. King's turn-about on the matter of gun legislation and his surrender to the hysteria which is currently sweeping the United States."[29] The relations between Loeb and King were to deteriorate further later in the campaign.

Although one cannot prove conclusively the existence of *Union Leader* influence in this case, King's behavior was consistent with the hypothesis that he carefully adopted—or at least *emphasized*—positions on issues which agreed with Loeb as long as King wanted to avoid the publisher's opposition; but once it became obvious that King would be opposed by the *Union Leader* no matter what he did, he no longer aligned his stands with those of the newspaper.

With the exception of the King-Cotton race in 1968, recent New Hampshire campaigns for the United States Senate do not present any obvious examples of candidates' changing their positions on national issues as a response to the *Union Leader*. Loeb-endorsed Senate candidates certainly have agreed with the publisher on the key issues; but reversal of positions has not been evident through the 1960–72 time period.

The newspaper may also help to determine which issues politicians decide to discuss in the first place. Former Concord lawyer and Democratic activist Eugene C. Struckhoff implies that both types of *Union Leader* influence operate:

When people decide, "How am I going to campaign?" and they say, "I can't *do* that, I mean you *can't* ask me to do that because if I do that I'm going to come up against Loeb". . . and say,

29. "Turncoat King," *Union Leader* (June 25, 1968), p. 1.

you know, "I'm going to go to Loeb and try to at least get him
to be neutral," . . . and actually talk with him—and then when
they decide what kind of an issue they're going to take to the
public now, they decide on the basis of what kind of response
are they going to get. In other words, how are they going to project this, are they going to be able to do it? . . . They don't take
the position on the basis whether they think there ought to be
public education of the voter towards this position; they make
the decision on the basis of "I can't take that position because
I'll get clobbered," you see. So I'm convinced that this is probably one of the most important influences. The negative, hidden
influence is every bit as important as whether Loeb elects a candidate or he doesn't elect a candidate.[30]

A case can be made that the *Union Leader* has played an important role in inducing gubernatorial candidates to discuss the tax
issue, which the interviewees unanimously agree has been the dominant issue in gubernatorial campaigns. As indicated above, the
Union Leader insists that candidates oppose the imposition of
new taxes by promising to veto such measures if elected governor.
This approach is illustrated by a 1968 editorial stating that the tax
issue cannot be compromised, adding: "And the ground rules call
for no less than unequivocal party opposition to the sales tax and,
on the part of candidates for governor, sincere pledges to veto either levy in the unlikely event it should receive legislative approval.
The people of New Hampshire have shown time and time again
that they will accept no less than the veto pledge."[31] In every gubernatorial campaign the *Union Leader* makes a great effort to
establish the "ground rules" in this way.

The *Union Leader*'s treatment of the tax issue helps to explain
the striking fact that it was the dominant issue even before 1966,
the first time a major candidate openly advocated a broad-base
tax.[32] Even if gubernatorial opponents both claimed to oppose
additional taxes, each candidate made considerable efforts to con-

30. Interview with Eugene C. Struckhoff, July 10, 1967.
31. "Moment of Truth," *Union Leader* (September 19, 1968).
32. In 1966 an openly protax position was taken by Alexander "Zandy"
Taft in the Republican primary. Taft was defeated and, as before, neither
gubernatorial nominee advocated a sales or income tax.

vince the public that he was more strongly against taxes. In an attempt to differentiate themselves from their competition, candidates who pledged to veto any new general tax legislation stressed this promise heavily, especially if their opponents refused to take the pledge (as in 1960 and 1966). Even when both candidates made the veto promise (as in 1962 and 1964), each urged that he was less of a "sales taxer"[33] than his opponent.

Thus by introducing and emphasizing the "pledge to veto" test, the *Union Leader* has fashioned a tool that has been used by candidates in their campaigns—originally by Loeb-supported Wesley Powell, later in 1962 by *Union Leader*-opposed John King, and more recently by other candidates. Perceiving the advantage of discussing the veto pledge, certain contenders have introduced the tax issue into the campaign. Loeb defines the topic in such a way as to create a distinction between certain candidates: not whether a politician says he opposes new taxes but whether he *pledges to veto* a sales or income tax,[34] and the pledge to veto becomes itself a new issue. Discussing the *Union Leader* and taxes, an adviser to former Governor King remarks, "They created the issue really almost out of thin air."[35]

Perhaps some candidate would have initiated the "veto pledge" test in the absence of the *Union Leader*, but even if a politician first introduced the tactic (I have no solid evidence that this was not the case), extensive *Union Leader* news and editorial publicity for the no-tax promise has increased the expected payoff of making the pledge. As for the anti-Loeb candidates, many of them have felt that they must respond to Loeb and not allow his arguments to go unanswered. In this way a dialogue on taxes has frequently taken place between the newspaper and one candidate, as well as between the candidates. Regardless of who gets primary

33. In 1967 I found that this term, coined and publicized by the *Union Leader*, was common in New Hampshire political discourse. By contrast, none of the Vermont interviewees used "sales taxer," despite the controversiality of the sales tax as a political issue in Vermont at that time.

Returning to New Hampshire in 1972, I discovered that "broad base taxer," which had replaced "sales taxer" as a favorite *Union Leader* term, had likewise replaced "sales taxer" in everyday political conversation.

34. Chapter 4 will examine the tax "issue definition" in greater detail.

35. Interview, not for attribution, September 6, 1967.

credit for initiating such discussions, *Union Leader* emphasis of
the tax issue and the veto pledge have certainly helped to *sustain*
the issue once it has entered the realm of public debate.

No other major issues appear to have been initiated or sustained
to a significant degree by the Loeb press. The interviewees did not
mention the pet *Union Leader* issues of the sweepstakes and the
ban on communist speakers as having been important in any campaign. The *Union Leader* has boosted these causes mainly during
legislative sessions and never made a systematic attempt to inject
them into election campaigns.

Retail price controls on milk is a possible example of an unsuccessful attempt by the Loeb press (especially the *Sunday News*) to
initiate a major issue. In 1958 Democratic gubernatorial candidate
Bernard L. Boutin was sharply criticized by the *Sunday News* for
his alleged opposition to the elimination of milk price controls. An
October 9, 1960, page one *Sunday News* headline proclaimed
"Milk Again N.H. Vote Issue" and stated that Governor Wesley
Powell, in contrast to Boutin, definitely believed that milk price
controls should be abolished. Despite this attempt and others to
create the issue, none of the interviewees referred to it as a major
campaign topic. Perhaps the politicians did not perceive enough
voter interest to make it a profitable issue. Even so, former Democratic National Committeeman William L. Dunfey says it had a
significant influence in bringing about Boutin's 1960 defeat.[36]
Boutin himself takes a contrasting view: "There was also a completely phony issue of milk control at that time [1960]. . . . It
hurt a little, but not very much."[37]

The history of the tax issue in gubernatorial campaigns suggests
that under favorable conditions the *Union Leader* can play a key
role in setting the campaign agenda—in helping to decide what

36. Interview with William L. Dunfey, September 12, 1967.
37. Interview with Bernard L. Boutin, April 20, 1968.

It is interesting to note that Keene *Sentinel* publisher James D. Ewing
reports (in his interview, September 8, 1967) that his paper campaigned for
the abolition of milk price controls before Loeb took up the issue. Nevertheless, none of the interviewees mentioned the *Sentinel* in connection with
milk control, though many referred to it as a pet issue ot Loeb's. This is a
small example of why the *Union Leader* is sometimes called the "dominant
voice" among New Hampshire newspapers.

issues are to be discussed, and on what terms. In addition, the Loeb press frequently injects minor topics of discussion into campaigns. Concerning Loeb, former Democratic National Committeeman Joseph A. Millimet asserts, "There's no doubt that he's had a great influence on the level of political discussion in New Hampshire. Whether he has succeeded in what he wants to support or not may be almost irrelevant because he tends to set the issues in New Hampshire."[38]

It is my distinct impression that most anti-Loeb candidates do not think very systematically prior to a campaign about how to structure the agenda themselves, rather than how to react to the *Union Leader's* agenda. An exception is Senator Thomas McIntyre, who very early prepared his strategy for the 1972 campaign by planning how to dominate the agenda with the issue of lower oil prices for New England consumers. A top McIntyre aide observes:

> My point is, [by emphasizing the oil issue] over four years, then when the *Union Leader* would want to come in and make the issue something else—you know, we had the knocko to come in and say no, the issue is oil. Then they have to relate to your issue, which is exactly what Loeb did five weeks after the primary. Now that took one hell of a lot of investment of effort and time. It wasn't just a political calculation, it was something that was a very valid policy issue the Senator had strong feelings on. It was valid, and that was the reason it had clout.[39]

The success of McIntyre's strategy was aided by the facts that he was the incumbent and that the *Union Leader* paid somewhat greater attention to the 1972 gubernatorial campaign compared with the senatorial contest.

Loeb As a Campaign Issue

The 1966 senatorial campaigns (above, Chapter 2) suggest that William Loeb might help to set the issue agenda by becoming a topic of campaign discussion himself. According to this pattern,

38. Interview with Joseph A. Millimet, August 28, 1967.
39. Interview, not for attribution, November 17, 1972.

the publisher is attacked by a candidate who chooses to emphasize the "Loeb issue" rather than other items.

Have anti-Loeb attacks been common in major New Hampshire
political campaigns? If so, has this approach played an integral
part in candidates' strategies, as in the case of Thomas McIntyre
in 1966 and to a lesser extent William Johnson that same year?
Let us examine the record.

Three interviewed candidates claimed that they were the first to
attack Loeb openly in a campaign. Actually, William Dunfey reports that the anti-Loeb tactic started with the late Senator Charles
Tobey in the Republican senatorial primary of 1950.[40] Tobey, an
outspoken liberal, was challenged by young Wesley Powell. Powell
received the support of Loeb, who had bought the *Union Leader*
in 1946. Loeb wrote some very sharp editorials attacking the incumbent Senator. According to Dunfey, Tobey criticized both
Powell and Loeb in the campaign. Tobey won narrowly and went
on to gain reelection.

In 1958 Powell won a bitter gubernatorial primary over Hugh
Gregg and faced Democrat Bernard Boutin in the general election.
The *Union Leader* ardently backed Powell and criticized his opponent. Boutin says that he answered Loeb's charges that he would
impose a sales tax if elected, and openly attacked the *Union Leader* publisher. According to Boutin, these anti-Loeb attacks became
"a principal ingredient" of his strategy late in the campaign.[41]
Powell narrowly defeated Boutin on election day. In 1960 Boutin
again criticized the *Union Leader* during the election campaign.
The Democrat lost by a wider margin than in 1958.

As the incumbent governor in 1960, Powell once more faced a
primary challenge from former Governor Gregg. Soon after Gregg
announced, Loeb attacked him as being the wealthy candidate of
the "Concord Gang," Loeb's term for the New Hampshire Republican establishment; by contrast, Loeb termed Powell the "cham-
pion of the average citizen of New Hampshire."[42] Later in the

40. Interview with William L. Dunfey, September 12, 1967.
41. Interview with Bernard L. Boutin, April 20, 1968.
42. "Gregg, Grudge Candidate," *Union Leader* (March 31, 1960), p. 1.
Other populistic-style attacks on Gregg were made in such front-page *Union
Leader* editorials as "Call Me Mister" (April 8) and "Our Lords and Masters"
(April 20).

campaign the publisher argued that Gregg intended to saddle the working people of New Hampshire with a sales tax, though Gregg denied advocating such a levy. Gregg responded by attacking Loeb and his newspaper. Comparing his tactics with those of McIntyre and Johnson, Gregg says that he attacked Loeb "with a lot more flourish . . . They didn't go after Loeb at all; I went after him in a big way." The former Governor recalls that he bought television time and showed photographs of Loeb's Massachusetts estate.[43] Gregg lost by a razor-thin margin to Powell, who went on to win his second term in November.

Ironically, Powell himself attacked Loeb in 1962 after the publisher had reversed his former support for the Governor. Loeb was also the object of attack in a primary-election-eve newspaper advertisement on behalf of senatorial candidate Perkins Bass. A third strong attack on Loeb by a 1962 candidate took place in the Republican Second Congressional District primary, which was discussed above with reference to the recruitment of Stacey Cole. Loeb blasted candidate James Cleveland in several editorials. The climax occurred in a front-page editorial headlined "Communism and Atheism," in which Loeb attacked Cleveland for having defended a communist as a lawyer and for supporting the Supreme Court's prayer ban decision. Loeb asked: "Do you want a man who, either willfully or through ignorance of the facts, aids the two forces of communism and atheism?"[44] Several days later Cleveland responded in a sharply worded reply: "Mr. Loeb, I did not crawl out of a foxhole in the Pacific Theater to come back home and crawl on my belly before a junior grade Goebbels whose combat experience has been chiefly confined to lawsuits and character assassinations!"[45] After one more response by the publisher, the Loeb-Cleveland verbal battle subsided for the rest of the campaign as Loeb concentrated on the gubernatorial and senatorial contests.

We have seen that Cleveland won the primary by a very slim margin over Bert Teague. Cleveland feels that his exchange with Loeb was helpful: "I think his attack on me did me much more

43. Interview with Hugh Gregg, July 24, 1967.
44. "Communism and Atheism," *Union Leader* (August 2, 1962), p.1.
45. Quoted in "Angry Cleveland Raps Opposition of Loeb," *Union Leader* (August 7, 1962), p. 1.

good than harm. . . . My rebuttal was a darn good one. It was
pretty strong, and it established among other things that—I think
I had something of a reputation as a state senator of being sort of
scholarly—but it proved among other things that when the situation called for it I was capable of fairly strong and forthright statements. And it rang a bell with a lot of people; I know that."[46]

A similar confrontation occurred in the 1964 general election
between Loeb and Democrat J. Oliva Huot, who upset incumbent
Congressman Louis C. Wyman. Loeb endorsed Wyman in his front-
page editorial "For God, Country and America":

> . . . it is quite clear from his votes that Louis Wyman believes in
> God and country. [The choice between Wyman and Huot] is a
> question of whether you want to save the United States in which
> we all believe. . . or whether you DON'T want to save the United
> States. If you believe in all these fundamental American ideas and
> ideals, then vote for Louis Wyman, if you don't so believe, then
> vote for Oliva Huot.[47]

Huot responded two days later, saying in part: "I am tired and I
am sure every citizen of the 1st District is tired of being called a
Socialist or Communist by William Loeb just because we do not
agree with him, or his philosophical twins, Barry Goldwater and
Louis Wyman. I would not think of calling Mr. Loeb a fascist
merely because his ideas are different than mine."[48]

In addition to McIntyre, Johnson, and Powell, Alexander M.
"Zandy" Taft criticized Loeb sharply during the 1966 campaign.
Taft, who finished third in the Republican gubernatorial primary,
had been taken to task by the *Union Leader* for openly advocating
a general sales or income tax.

As noted above, Loeb and Governor John King, who had agreed
on the issues most important to the *Union Leader*, began to oppose
each other in 1968 when King ran for the Senate against Loeb-supported incumbent Norris Cotton. In early October, Loeb claimed

46. Interview with James C. Cleveland, September 26, 1967.
47. "For God, Country and America," *Union Leader* (October 19,1964), p. 1.
48. Quoted in "Huot Criticizes Publisher Loeb's Editorial Policy," *Union
Leader* (October 21, 1964), p. 1.

that a King advertisement about Cotton's record was "a gross misrepresentation, if not a downright lie."[49] King responded, in part, "Having a hard time to find anything wrong with my record as Governor of New Hampshire, Mr. Loeb, in his usual fashion, has taken vitriolic attacks on my person by name calling."[50] Two weeks later Loeb again accused King of distorting Cotton's record and asserted, "Apparently, just as Adolf Hitler and the Communists specialize in The Big Lie, Gov. King thinks this is the way to get himself elected—tell enough lies enough times and people are supposed to believe him."[51] King then called a press conference to launch a strong attack on Loeb, and the *Union Leader* printed the Governor's remarks together with additional charges by the publisher.[52]

Announcing for reelection in 1970, Republican Governor Walter R. Peterson was asked what the main issue would be in his campaign. He responded: "Well, I think in any campaign in New Hampshire the issue actually is between William Loeb and me."[53] Loeb reacted by stating what he thought of candidates' attempts to make him a campaign issue:

Governor Peterson says the issue of this campaign is going to be William Loeb. Well, good luck to him. Bill Johnson used that issue and he lost. John King used that issue and HE lost. McIntyre used the issue and he won, but only because his opponent was as inarticulate as he was modest and heroic in the defense of his nation in time of war. . . .

The REAL issue, Governor Peterson, is whether you and other scheming politicians will control the state of New Hampshire for the benefit of yourself and your pals. So stop trying to throw political dust in the eyes of the voters by making attacks on the

49. "Thou Shalt Not Lie!" *Union Leader* (October 7, 1968), p. 1.

50. Quoted in "Sen. Cotton, Loeb Assailed by King," *Union Leader* (October 15, 1968), p. 1.

51. "Come Up out of the Mud, Governor!" *Union Leader* (October 30, 1968), p. 1.

52. "King Labels Union Leader 'Evil'—Loeb Sees JWK 'Desperate,' " *Union Leader* (November 1, 1968), p. 3.

53. Quoted in "Governor Peterson Seeks Second Term," *Union Leader* (July 15, 1970), p. 1.

Manchester *Union*, the New Hampshire *Sunday News* and the publisher and editors.[54]

Evidently Peterson had second thoughts about making Loeb a major issue, for he did not raise the subject again during the campaign.

In 1972 Democratic candidates Thomas McIntyre and Robert Raiche both made isolated attacks on Loeb,[55] but no candidates that year attempted to make the publisher a main topic of campaign discussion.

We have seen that a variety of candidates have attacked Loeb: Democrats and Republicans, candidates in primaries and general elections, winners and losers. Do any basic patterns emerge from these cases?

Candidates tend to react to criticism from Loeb, rather than seizing the initiative. Loeb makes a series of attacks against a candidate; the politician usually responds; but when the publisher refrains from blasting the candidate in his page-one editorials, the politician does not attack the *Union Leader*. Thus Loeb generally holds the initiative in determining whether the publisher becomes a prominent topic of discussion in the campaign.

Senator McIntyre is an example of a candidate whose use of the anti-Loeb tactic is at least partially contingent on the actions of the publisher. Although McIntyre battled Loeb openly in 1966, he refrained from such activity in the 1962 special election. Speaking in 1967, a McIntyre staff member suggested that the crucial difference between these two cases was that while the *Union Leader* ardently opposed the Senator in 1966, "In 1962 we didn't have much of a problem with Loeb because Loeb's attitude in 1962 was 'a curse on both your houses.' He didn't like Perkins Bass any more than he liked Tom McIntyre. And he concentrated in that year on other campaigns more than on ours."[56] In the same way, Hugh Gregg attacked Loeb in 1960 when the publisher opposed

54. "The Real Issue," *Union Leader* (July 15, 1970), p. 1.

55. For example, see "Sen. McIntyre Attacks Loeb," *Union Leader* (September 29, 1972), p.1, and "Raiche Delivers Blast at Loeb," ibid. (August 18, 1972), p. 1.

56. Interview, not for attribution, September 28, 1967.

him but held his fire in the 1966 general election when Loeb was neutral.

Similarly, Governor King did not criticize Loeb publicly as long as the publisher avoided attacking the Governor. In 1967 a top Democratic adviser confided: "[In 1966] John King didn't denounce Loeb because he wasn't hurting John. But you can't say that the next election we would do the same thing. He might knife John King the next time around. Supposing John King were to decide to run for the Senate. Then Loeb might knife him because he might want Cotton, you see. And so you might have to treat him in a different way."[57] We have seen that this 1968 confrontation did take place, with King engaging Loeb in acrimonious dispute.

A few candidates who have been attacked by the *Union Leader* had previously tried to induce such criticism. An example is reported by Herbert Hill, the Democratic senatorial nominee in 1960. Hill states that he made a foreign policy statement designed in part to antagonize Loeb and attract the publicity that would follow in a page-one *Leader* editorial.[58] Loeb did not respond, however, and Hill failed to become embroiled in a public confrontation with the publisher. In some isolated instances this tactic may have succeeded in starting a debate with Loeb; nevertheless, the safe generalization is that Loeb, rather than the candidate, initiates direct arguments between the newspaper and the politician.

The usual pattern is that a candidate who is not actively supported by the *Leader* hopes the paper will not oppose him because it has a net-positive impact on the voters, and because of the desire to avoid that type of personal attack. Once the newspaper starts to criticize the candidate strongly, however, the situation changes. Continuing to say nothing about Loeb or the paper apparently will not induce the *Leader* to cease its attacks; damage has already been done and will probably continue to be done. However, the candidate has the opportunity to cut his losses and pick up some mileage by responding to Loeb. First, the politician can gain the sympathy of the elements of the public and the press which react strongly against Loeb per se. Second, the candidate can reap the

57. Interview with Joseph A. Millimet, August 28, 1967.
58. Conversation with Herbert Hill, February 16, 1967.

benefits of publicity flowing from his anti-Loeb statement, publicity which includes the usual front-page *Leader* coverage of an exchange between a candidate and Loeb. Third, a heated encounter with Loeb can be used by the candidate as a means of projecting a vigorous image, as James Cleveland tried to do in 1962.

On the other hand, responding with an anti-Loeb blast carries with it certain potential drawbacks. In a debate with a newspaper, the paper is always able to have the final say in its pages; a candidate's attack may increase the probability that the newspaper will give him unfavorable news and editorial coverage. A politician may feel that his image of responsibility and moderation will suffer if he engages in a bitter dispute with Loeb. Finally, he must consider whether he wants to subject himself to the additional personal abuse that may flow after an anti-Loeb attack but not otherwise.

In weighing these factors, the great majority of candidates who have been assailed by Loeb have concluded that the wisest course of action is to attack Loeb publicly and strongly.

The above discussion is framed in terms of dealing with virulent and/or sustained attacks by Loeb. But what if the publisher criticizes the politician less intensively? In such cases the most common reaction has been to ignore Loeb or else to criticize him but not heatedly. Senator McIntyre's behavior in 1972 is a good example of this pattern: having been criticized but not really blasted by Loeb, McIntyre made one sharp attack on Loeb but did not belabor the point as he had in 1966. In the same way, Robert Raiche reacted to relatively mild Loeb criticism by making low-key anti-Loeb comments while campaigning. Raiche reports that prior to the campaign he and his advisers seriously considered attacking the *Union Leader* on a sustained basis; but they decided not to under the assumption that a fight with Loeb would hurt Raiche's image by lowering him to a name-calling level.[59]

Likewise, during the 1972 Republican gubernatorial primary Governor Peterson was occasionally criticized by Loeb, but not nearly so frequently nor sharply as in previous years. In response, Peterson made no well-publicized attacks on Loeb. Asked whether the Governor wanted to engage Loeb in a public fight, Peterson

59. Interview with Robert E. Raiche, October 13, 1972.

aide David Hess replies, "No. I think the general consensus was, you never win that type of a fight with Loeb—because he always gets the final word in the newspaper. And Peterson had the name recognition already, so you don't need negative publicity to get name recognition."[60] A relatively unknown candidate, then, may want to draw *Union Leader* criticism in order to gain publicity, and this line of reasoning was central to William Johnson's decision to attack Loeb in 1966.

A further refinement is that candidates are concerned mostly about responding to Loeb's highly visible front-page editorials. Not one of those interviewed mentioned the possibility of answering the inside editorials.

In reviewing the cases of candidates' anti-Loeb appeals, one should distinguish pre- and post-1966 instances from the activities of Johnson and McIntyre that year. Those two candidates utilized the anti-Loeb maneuver as an integral part of their overall strategies, though Johnson's anti-Loeb statements were confined almost entirely to the first two weeks of a long primary campaign. But other attacks on Loeb have been relatively low-level activities and are tactics rather than strategies. Candidates have responded to the *Union Leader* publisher, but rarely have anti-Loeb approaches been a major thrust in a campaign strategy. For example, a 1967 interview suggests that Oliva Huot's heated exchange with Loeb in 1964[61] was not a salient part of the campaign for him:

> Q. Did the *Union Leader* get very involved in your campaign, in your congressional race in 1964?
>
> A. No, I would say that they did not. I think that they gave us coverage. I'm not sure that they took a real strong editorial position. They may have said that they were for Wyman; I really don't recall that.[62]

With respect to a broad anti-Loeb strategy, who in general can gain most from this approach, Democratic candidates or Republicans? In primaries or in general elections? Responses to these ques-

60. Interview with David Hess, September 29, 1972.
61. The Loeb editorial "For God, Country and America" and Huot's response, cited above.
62. Interview with J. Oliva Huot, September 29, 1967.

tions contain internal contradictions, indicating that even some of
the more astute Democratic and Republican strategic thinkers
have not carefully formulated theories about who should or should
not attack the *Union Leader*. The following points were made:

Democratic candidates can afford to engage Loeb in public battle,
particularly in general elections. The reasoning is that a Democratic candidate does not need the conservative vote that is presumably influenced positively by the *Union Leader*. The assumption
is made that Democratic voters are less conservative than Republicans and thus are influenced by Loeb to a lesser extent. On the
other hand, *Union Leader* circulation and, presumably, influence
are greatest in Manchester. This Democratic stronghold is particularly vital in a Democratic primary, in which Manchester accounts
for a larger percentage of the vote than the city contributes in a
Republican primary or in a general election. Moreover, perhaps
Republican voters are *not* influenced more than Democrats by the
Union Leader; former Democratic National Committeeman Joseph
A. Millimet says: "Strangely enough, I think that Loeb's techniques have more influence on Democrats than on Republicans—
by and large. Let's not kid ourselves: by and large Republicans are
richer than Democrats. They usually have had more education.
They're likely to be more sophisticated on things of this nature
and less likely to be taken in by people like Loeb."[63] It is relevant
to point out that although Loeb has endorsed more Republicans
than Democrats, he has refrained from making partisan appeals
that might alienate Democratic voters. Considerations of this sort
lead to the conclusion that a Democratic candidate risks losing a
good deal by systematically attacking Loeb, especially in primaries.

Similar reasoning focused on Republican candidates, however,
can lead to the conclusions that it is either more or less advanta-
geous for a member of the GOP than a Democrat to become an
anti-Loeb candidate. For example, one argument asserts that a
Republican needs conservative support in the general election and
will lose this backing if he openly opposes Loeb. On the other
hand, a Republican might be able to antagonize Loeb because he

63. Interview with Joseph A. Millimet, August 28, 1967.

could gain some anti-Loeb Democratic votes and will not lose the Republican right, which will not swing to the Democrat unless he is an unusually conservative candidate.

Several interviewees hold the view that blanket generalizations on the wisdom of an anti-Loeb strategy are difficult to make. The advisability of this approach depends on particular circumstances, such as the number of opponents (in a primary), the nature of the opposition, and the agenda of campaign issues.

An evaluation of the logic of McIntyre's and Johnson's anti-Loeb strategies should consider the candidates' assumption that a sharp attack on the *Union Leader* publisher would produce a favorable reaction from most of the evening dailies. These two candidates are satisfied that this calculation was correct. And the feeling is widespread among the interviewed politicians that such an "anti-Loeb reflex" is common for the non-*Union Leader* newspapers; one Democrat says the latter sometimes react "almost in a pavlovian fashion" against Loeb.[64]

However, a contrary view is taken by several people, including James D. Ewing, publisher of the Keene *Sentinel*. Ewing claims that there is "almost no merit" to the belief that evening dailies react against Loeb per se. Rather, Ewing believes, the moderate New Hampshire press takes positions contrary to Loeb's on many issues; but there is no causal link between these editorial decisions of different papers.[65] Any overall generalization on the hypothesized "anti-Loeb reflex" fails to take into account the range in behavior of the evening moderate press. In fact, some editorial pages rarely respond to the *Union Leader*, while others frequently attack Loeb. At any rate, the politicians interviewed, whether they supported or opposed Thyng, all state that in 1966 a general and strong anti-Loeb reaction in the evening press was skillfully cultivated by Johnson and McIntyre.

Although occasional attacks on William Loeb and the *Union Leader* will probably continue to occur in New Hampshire political campaigns, it seems unlikely that Loeb and the paper will be a dominant issue except in extraordinary circumstances. We have

64. Interview, not for attribution, September 6, 1967.
65. Interview with James D. Ewing, September 8, 1967.

seen that the 1966 senatorial campaigns were extraordinary because of the nature of General Thyng as a politically inexperienced
candidate, virtually unknown aside from the *Union Leader*. In this
sense Thyng was the perfect target for the anti-Loeb strategy, especially McIntyre's "Loeb puppet" theme. The charge was credible
when used against Thyng and Loeb, but such attacks on most
Loeb-backed candidates would look foolish and artificial. Since
I expect few candidates of the future to be inexperienced, *Union
Leader* influence over the political agenda will be largely confined
to more conventional issues, such as taxes.

Influence Bases of the Union Leader

Insofar as the *Union Leader* influences candidates' strategies and
activities, *why* is this the case? Why do politicians take the *Union
Leader* into account when they decide how to campaign? In other
words, what are the "influence bases" of the newspaper with respect to politicians' decisions?[66] In answering these questions, I
shall draw on limited comparative material from Vermont in order
to illuminate the New Hampshire situation.

An obvious and extremely important reason why candidates may
be influenced by a newspaper is their belief that the paper has a
significant impact on the electorate. The strong consensus of the
interviewed New Hampshire politicians, of both parties and with
varying political views, is that the *Union Leader* is an important
influence on voters. Indeed, when I asked whether the Loeb press
exerts a significant force on its readers in the direction of Loeb-
supported candidates, the interviewees' answers often indicated
that they thought the question was silly or trivial: *of course* the
Union Leader is an important influence on the electorate. For example, William Johnson states that most New Hampshire candidates "think that Loeb is a key factor in winning elections. And
of course he is. That's a simple fact of life. He is. He is a very important factor in winning elections."[67]

66. Cf. the Lasswell and Kaplan definition of a base value in an influence
relationship. Harold D. Lasswell and Abraham Kaplan, *Power and Society*
(New Haven: Yale University Press, 1950), p. 83.
67. Interview with William R. Johnson, July 31, 1967.

One indication of the perceived impact of a newspaper on voters is the belief by candidates that the editorial endorsement of the paper is a helpful factor. Most of the interviewed New Hampshire politicians believe that overall, *Union Leader* support for any candidate wins that man more votes than such backing loses. Therefore, candidates presumably would rather have Loeb's editorial blessing than not have it. Bert F. Teague, a candidate for the Republican Second District congressional nomination in 1954 and 1962, asserts: "If you find a candidate—a present candidate, a present incumbent, a future candidate, or a past candidate—who will tell you that he wouldn't take the support of the *Union Leader* if he could have it—*if he could have it*—I'll show you the biggest hypocrite that's ever been in New Hampshire politics."[68] In the subsequent discussion with Teague, it became clear he meant that *any* candidate would rather have Loeb's support than not have it—but that the question is academic once it becomes obvious Loeb will oppose the candidate.

To say that candidates perceive *Union Leader* support to be beneficial on the whole, however, is not to say that politicians perceive all of the paper's editorials to have only a positive impact. We have seen that Johnson calculated that his attacks on Loeb would give him the votes of a number of people who react extremely negatively to the *Union Leader* publisher. We have also noted the feeling among several politicians that some individual Loeb editorials are harmful for his candidate, particularly strong personal attacks on opponents. A Manchester Democratic officeholder states that such Loeb attacks "go against our system of fair play" and are resented by many voters.[69] The 1966 Vermont Republican gubernatorial candidate Richard A. Snelling, exposed to Loeb through the Vermont *Sunday News*, says:

> I would say that on balance having the support of the editor of any newspaper is helpful except in very extraordinary circumstances—which is not to say that a given editorial or a given statement in support of you might not cause harm, if it is strident or unfair in its attacks on your opponent. . . . You know,

68. Interview with Bert F. Teague, July 27, 1967.
69. Interview, not for attribution, July 13, 1967.

Loeb: insulting people terribly, using words like "idiot" about public figures, and so on. I think probably it alienates more people to his point of view and therefore creates some sympathy for the candidate.[70]

Such Loeb editorials also give publicity to the attacked candidate. Former Democratic National Committeeman Joseph A. Millimet comments, "He [Loeb] is certainly no unmixed blessing to have on your side."[71]

Are there any candidates who might have had a chance to obtain Loeb's editorial backing but still preferred not to receive it? In 1967 a close associate of Governor King stated:

A. We don't want his [Loeb's] endorsement, necessarily. Well, not—we don't want his endorsement, period.

Q. Why is that?

A. Because there are many thousands of people in the state of New Hampshire who will vote against a man simply because he is endorsed by the *Union Leader*.

Q. Do you think this would outweigh the positive benefits?

A. It very well could. In fact, I have the impression that they almost cancel each other out.[72]

On the other hand, King preferred not to be attacked by the *Union Leader*, either. Since his home town was Manchester, perhaps he felt less dependent than non-Manchester candidates on the support of that city's newspaper in order to do well there.

If we distinguish between news coverage and editorial support, the following generalizations can be made: candidates unanimously desire favorable *Union Leader* news coverage—which, as we shall see in Chapter 5, tends to be much more favorable if the candidate is backed editorially by the paper. On the other hand, Loeb editorial support per se carries with it some disadvantages; but the great majority of candidates prefer to have such backing than not to receive it. The interviews also strongly support the hypothesis that New Hampshire candidates would rather have the backing of the *Union Leader* than any other paper.

70. Interview with Richard A. Snelling, January 19, 1968.
71. Interview with Joseph A. Millimet, August 28, 1967.
72. Interview, not for attribution, September 6, 1967.

As a contrast, I draw on my handful of Vermont interviews (conducted mainly in 1967). Compared with the New Hampshire interviewees' views of the Loeb papers, there was much more questioning among Vermont candidates concerning the value of being endorsed by the state's two major dailies, the Burlington *Free Press* and the Rutland *Herald*. Doubts were raised especially about the value of *Free Press* backing; several interviewees stated that the Burlington newspaper has a poor reputation in its community and that it is helpful *not* to be supported by the paper. Such views should probably be taken with a grain of salt, however, as there was a tendency for candidates to dismiss the value of papers endorsing their opponents but to attribute positive influence to favorable papers.

Former Vermont Governor Philip H. Hoff is an example of a candidate who said he preferred to do without *Free Press* endorsement. Speaking in 1967, Hoff observed: "The Burlington *Free Press* was against me [in 1966]. And I think that helped me, not hurt me, because the editorial page has so little respect. . . . The *Free Press* editorial policy quite frankly is terrible. That's the only way you can describe it. . . . Now the support of the Rutland *Herald*, which does have a good reputation, for example, I think was helpful. Particularly since it was a Republican paper and it never endorsed a Democrat for the governorship before."[73] Hoff aide Benjamin Collins asserted: "Our feeling is, if we're for it and the *Free Press* is against it, we're in luck."[74] Perhaps liberal candidates like Hoff prefer not to be endorsed by a newspaper with a conservative reputation like the *Free Press*. Asked whether this is an accurate statement, *Free Press* editor Gordon Mills replies: "No. They'll say this, but I don't believe they believe it."[75]

In analyzing the desirability of endorsements, former *Free Press* political reporter and columnist Vic Maerki suggests that editorials can be helpful when they unexpectedly back a candidate—but that even then there is a possible backlash:

Like most newspapers, the *Free Press* editorial position is very

73. Interview with Philip H. Hoff, November 21, 1967.
74. Interview with Benjamin Collins, November 10, 1967.
75. Interview with Gordon Mills, December 19, 1967.

predictable. . . . Therefore, I think that nobody's surprised or unduly influenced when they see the *Free Press* come out for the conservative Republican businessman running against the liberal Democrat. However, what would happen if the *Free Press* came out and endorsed the liberal Democrat running against the conservative Republican businessman? The first thing that would happen, most people would say, "My God, how come they are endorsing him?" And I think you get two reactions out of this. One, this liberal Democrat must be an unusually good character to get *Free Press* support because generally he doesn't stand for what they stand for. So he must be so exceptional that they're waiving their positional stand here. Or, two, maybe this fellow's not quite the liberal Democrat that we thought he is if he gets the *Free Press* support. And in this case I think there have been some candidates who would appreciate no *Free Press* endorsement because it would raise the question of what they think is their legitimate position. Most of the candidates I've talked to, though, would like *Free Press* endorsement of their stands on issues.[76]

In many situations, then, the desirability of a blanket endorsement may be a complex function of the ideological reputations of the candidate and the newspaper, together with the candidate's view of which ideological groups he would most like to attract in the campaign. But almost no New Hampshire interviewees mentioned such qualifications in discussing the value of *Union Leader* endorsement.

To this point the main conclusion has been that the support of the *Union Leader* is perceived by candidates to be valuable, more so than the support of other papers. One reason why some politicians have this perception is that they interpret election patterns as indicating *Union Leader* influence over voters. For example, former Governor Peterson states: "If you study the election returns, both in primaries and in elections, in the areas where the *Union Leader* runs and is not contested by another newspaper, an afternoon daily that might represent a different view—in those areas the *Union Leader* sweeps, you see. When you get into the other sec- ·

76. Interview with Vic Maerki, December 13, 1967.

tions—if you go down the Connecticut River valley, if you get into
the seacoast area, to a degree around Nashua, certainly around
Concord—then you get a different picture, where this condition
stops and you see voting results that are markedly different."[77]
Chapter 5 will examine newspaper circulation and voting patterns
to assess the accuracy of this kind of observation.

Perhaps certain characteristics of newspapers directly induce the
perception of electoral influence. We would expect that, other
things equal, the larger the number of editorials a newspaper usually devotes to an election campaign, the more influential the
paper is perceived as being. In explaining why the editorial support
of one paper is more highly desired than the backing of other papers, the frequency and strength of editorials could be an important variable.

A comparison between the Manchester *Union Leader* and the
Burlington *Free Press* suggests that with circulation held constant,
the more vigorous and frequent a paper's political editorials are,
the more pronounced its perceived impact on the electorate. The
Union Leader and the *Free Press* have about the same circulation,
as measured by percentage of total daily newspaper circulation in
a state;[78] and the *Free Press* is far less vigorous in its political advocacy than the *Union Leader*. There was a dissensus among the interviewed Vermont politicians regarding the value of *Free Press*
editorial support, but not a single New Hampshire political figure
called the *Union Leader* unimportant in influencing voters. This
perceived value of *Union Leader* backing is based in large part on

77. Interview with Walter Peterson, December 8, 1972.

78. Forty percent for the *Union Leader*, 36 percent for the *Free Press*
(1966); 38 percent for both (1972). This calculation includes only the daily
newspapers published in each state and assumes that all circulation is confined to the state of publication. However, there is one exception to this
procedure: the Lebanon-White River Junction *Valley News* is the only paper
with a significant proportion of its circulation in both states. Projecting the
proportion of 1964 *Valley News* circulation in New Hampshire and Vermont,
I estimated the paper's circulation in the two states for 1966 and 1972. The
1964 source is *American Newspaper Markets' Circulation '64* (Northfield,
Ill.: American Newspaper Markets, Inc.). The source for the 1966 and 1972
circulation figures is *Editor and Publisher International Year Book*, 1967,
1973.

its news coverage, but the Loeb editorial "treatment" was also mentioned often as being a significant factor. Not surprisingly, the intensity of a newspaper's advocacy (whether in editorials or news columns) appears to be a key variable in explaining how influential the paper is thought to be by candidates.

That conclusion is buttressed by the New Hampshire interviewees' comparisons between the *Union Leader* and the other dailies in the state. These politicians often noted the difference between Loeb's day-in, day-out support for or attacks on a candidate and the lack of such crusading by the other newspapers. William Johnson, for example, says that he has told non-Loeb editors: "You know, you people are the kind of guys who think that when you endorse a politician on Thursday prior to the election on Tuesday—that's that—you've really done him a great favor. What you don't recognize is in the meantime that Bill Loeb may be endorsing his opponent. But he doesn't do it once; he does it fourteen, fifteen, eighteen, twenty times, on page one. In the meantime he kicks your candidate in the fanny ten times by saying what an S.O.B. he is."[79] Johnson, however, does not downgrade the collective impact of the "moderate" press, as we have seen with respect to his 1966 campaign strategy.

The following response by a McIntyre staff member is illustrative:

Q. Do you think that generally these other papers have as much influence in their areas as the *Union Leader* does in its area?

A. I think some of them do; some of them definitely do have. Some of them have little or no political impact in their community. They are not politically oriented; they devote very little space to political campaigns. Some of them, however, devote a good deal of space. The Portsmouth *Herald*, for example, is an activist newspaper in every sense of the word when it comes to politics and government. The Claremont *Daily Eagle* is, the Concord *Monitor* is. Some of the others—the Lebanon newspaper, for example—I think less so.[80]

79. Interview with William R. Johnson, September 16, 1967.
80. Interview, not for attribution, September 28, 1967.

It is interesting that this man seems to identify extent of political impact with extent of political activism in newspaper content.

The present argument has been that with circulation strength held constant, the perception of a newspaper's electoral impact varies directly with the vigor of the paper's political advocacy. Another comparison argues that if editorial intensity is held constant, greater perceived influence on the electorate is a positive function of larger circulation. This unsurprising conclusion is supported by a comparison between William Loeb's two large-circulation New Hampshire newspapers (the *Union Leader* and *Sunday News*) and his two smaller-circulation Vermont papers, the St. Albans *Messenger* and the Vermont *Sunday News*. Loeb's brand of political advocacy is found both in his New Hampshire and in his Vermont papers, though the latter carry fewer of his front-page editorials. We have argued that New Hampshire candidates agree overwhelmingly that the Loeb papers in their state are important in influencing voters. The interviewed Vermont politicians, however, are unanimous in dismissing the electoral importance of Loeb's Vermont papers.

There are possible weaknesses in our present argument that vigorous advocacy and circulation strength contribute to the perception of a newspaper's electoral importance if one or the other factor is held constant. First, with regard to vigorous advocacy, it is possible that our comparison between the *Union Leader* and the *Free Press* does not hold circulation strength constant. True, the two papers' percentages of total daily circulation in their respective states are about the same. But another way of measuring circulation strength is the ratio between the circulation of the largest and second-largest newspapers in a state. According to this alternative measure, the *Union Leader* is in a more dominant circulation position than the *Free Press*.[81] Moreover, perceived *Union Leader* circulation might be magnified because the newspaper is distributed throughout New Hampshire; when discussing the Manchester paper, many interviewees observed that it is "the only statewide daily." On the other hand, the *Free Press* circulates only

81. The 1966 ratios are 3.5 for the *Union Leader* and 1.8 for the *Free Press*; the 1972 ratios are, respectively, 2.8 and 2.0. Again the source is *Editor and Publisher International Year Book*, 1967, 1973.

around Burlington and in neighboring areas of northern Vermont.

In the same way, the comparison between Loeb's New Hampshire papers and his Vermont papers does not really hold degree of advocacy constant, since Loeb's attempts to persuade are printed more frequently in his New Hampshire papers than in his Vermont papers. Thus part of the reason the Loeb newspapers are perceived as being more influential in New Hampshire may be that Loeb's advocacy is more blatant than in Vermont.

Regarding the importance of circulation and perceived voter impact, a dissenting voice is raised by Clifton R. Noyes, editor of the St. Albans *Messenger* and Vermont *Sunday News*. In his 1972 interview, Noyes expressed the following opinions:

> I don't think [candidates] really give a damn or really know about circulation. I think they're concerned with a loud voice; you know, it's the same old story about the wheel that squeaks the loudest gets the most grease. I think it's a question of just the possibility of us feeding stuff out that somebody's going to pick up and it's going to go on from there. I don't think it's a circulation problem, no. . . .

> Again—you speak about circulation and the Manchester paper and circulation and our paper, and so on—I really don't believe that the candidates are as concerned about the circulation as they are about the editorial being written, whether it's one or a thousand and one or 63,000. A large number of candidates will do all they can to avoid a confrontation, to avoid a blistering editorial, and I think circulation's the farthest thing from their mind. . . .

> I think with the Manchester *Union Leader* that sometimes circulation is overemphasized. I think if it were a local paper in the city of Manchester and had 20 or 30 thousand circulation, you'd still hear all the agonizing noises from the candidates—because a candidate just doesn't like to fall victim to harsh criticism. And I think that we can cite our Sunday paper here as the best example, because we're number three on the ladder in circulation—but if they feel there's a critical edit coming, then officeholders

and candidates will usually do their utmost to (as they put it) set the record straight.[82]

Although I think that Noyes underestimates the importance of circulation strength as a condition for direct influence on a candidate, he draws attention to a key mechanism through which a small newspaper can have an impact: by anticipating that larger newspapers or other media might disseminate a critical editorial or story printed by a small paper, a candidate may strive to avoid being attacked by the small paper and shape his actions accordingly.

In sum, intensity of political advocacy and circulation strength contribute positively and independently to candidates' perceptions of a newspaper's impact on the electorate. Such a perception is a significant influence base for a newspaper, Noyes' analysis notwithstanding.

Besides perceived impact on voters, a second possible base is the desire of candidates to avoid William Loeb's vitriolic editorial attacks. Above I discussed the dislike of personal attack as a factor weighing against some potential candidates' running in the first place. I would like to elaborate on this mechanism of Loeb influence.

The interviewees registered overwhelming agreement that dislike of personal attack per se—aside from anticipation of the *Union Leader's* electoral effects—is indeed a highly significant factor in explaining how Loeb enters their calculations.[83] Discussing elected officials as well as other candidates, William Johnson observes:

A. One of my favorite theories is that unlike what most people think, that politicians are thick-skinned, by and large they are very thin-skinned. The person that is literally thick-skinned, he wouldn't care what people thought of him and therefore wouldn't be very responsive and wouldn't be a very good politician. And only a person who is sensitive and thin-skinned and tries to please, works to please and so forth, can really be a representa-

82. Interview with Clifton R. Noyes, August 29, 1972.
83. In questioning candidates on this point, I worded the query so as to apply *generally* to other politicians, not to the interviewee himself.

tive of the people because he tries so hard to get their approval. So I think what Bill Loeb does and why he gets much more influence than probably he merits is because he is so vigorous in his attacks that the average thin-skinned guy who gets very far in politics hates to see himself attacked. He hates to go downtown and spend a dime and buy a paper and find himself being attacked. And that, I think, is what does it more than anything else.

Q. Do you think that's more important than the politician rationally calculating the voter impact of the paper?

A. Sure, look—[Officeholder X] is a terribly sensitive guy, terribly sensitive. [Officeholder Y] is a very sensitive person. [Officeholder Z] is afraid of his own shadow. . . . When they buy a paper and they see themselves vigorously attacked, it tears them apart. And most newspapers think twice or three times before they really tear after somebody in public life. But Loeb thinks about half a second.[84]

Former Democratic National Committeeman William L. Dunfey analyzes Loeb's influence in a way consistent with Johnson's theory:

People who make some sort of career out of running for public office and being in public office look almost to the extreme for approval; they really do. I mean they have difficulty taking constructive criticism after they're in; and when they consider some of this not constructive even but destructive criticism, this kind of overwhelms them. . . . It's a strange thing, and if you talk to public figures you find out. The attrition that takes place with a guy, with his family, with his friends, on the type of assault that can go on really wears the hell out of them.[85]

Another former Democratic National Committeeman, Joseph A. Millimet, reports: "I've been attacked by him [Loeb] many times and I tell you, it's a very unpleasant experience. . . . Even though everybody who knows you or who knows the facts of the case knows that he is wrong, still in all, it's very unpleasant to see your

84. Interview with William R. Johnson, September 16, 1967.
85. Interview with William L. Dunfey, September 12, 1967.

name in the paper with some of the vituperation that he puts in. And nobody likes it."[86] Concerning candidates, though, Millimet suggests that dislike of being attacked is a less important factor in decisionmaking than the calculation of voter reaction. This observation appears to hold for Senator McIntyre's behavior in 1966.

As the above quotes indicate, the interviewees feel that the desire to avoid bitter personal attack is something candidates take into account in planning their actions and is therefore a potential influence base for the *Union Leader*. In the process of making decisions, however, other factors may override the force of avoiding destructive criticism. In particular, it is difficult to assess the relative importance of (a) calculation of newspaper effects on the electorate and (b) the desire to avert strong personal attack as influence bases of the *Union Leader*. The weighing of these factors is especially difficult because in most cases they point in the same direction: try not to antagonize Loeb.

A dissenting voice on the possible importance of desire to avoid personal attack is raised by Loeb himself:

Q. . . . I'm curious about your reaction to this possibility, in other words, that some candidates may be dissuaded from running because they fear that they would be attacked in print by the *Union Leader* or maybe that some candidates who are actually running may be influenced in some way during the campaign?

A. Gee, I would be awfully surprised. Wouldn't you think that would be an awfully timid kind of a candidate? You know what I mean; I can't imagine somebody saying, "I'm not going to run because I don't want to get hit in the rear." I should say such a person shouldn't—you know, as Harry Truman said—such a person shouldn't be in politics or even think about politics to begin with.

Q. Is it your impression, then, that politicians in New Hampshire actually are not that sensitive?

A. I don't think they're that sensitive or that fearful, either.[87]

Loeb's image of politicians thus contrasts with the Dunfey-Johnson

86. Interview with Joseph A. Millimet, August 28, 1967.
87. Interview with William Loeb, October 23, 1967.

conception. And the *Union Leader* publisher's view of the significance of candidates' desires to avoid his barbs also runs against the
prevailing opinion of the interviewed politicians.

Loeb has also inserted his personal brand of invective into his
Vermont newspapers. But in contrast with the New Hampshire
candidates, the interviewed Vermont politicians unanimously dismiss the possibility that the desire to avoid Loeb's attacks influences candidates in any way. For example, one recent candidate
asserts:

A. I think politicians as a group are a gutless bunch. And I
think that they die inside if they think some newspaper's going
to say something unpleasant about them or that an editorial will
attack them. . . .

Q. And with regard to Loeb's paper in particular, do you feel
that it has impact in this manner?

A. Generally little in this case. . . . I don't think anybody really
pays much attention to Loeb's newspapers.[88]

This opinion certainly contradicts editor Clifton Noyes' belief
that statewide candidates are concerned about Loeb's Vermont
papers. But it seems safe to argue that New Hampshire candidates
are much more worried about being attacked by the Loeb press
than Vermont candidates are concerned about the Vermont *Sunday News* and St. Albans *Messenger*. If this proposition is correct,
why do politicians pay less attention to Loeb's Vermont newspapers? One strong possibility is that they perceive these papers
as having relatively little influence with the electorate because of
their small circulation. Assuming that few people read the papers
(and perhaps not always reading them themselves), the Vermont
politicians are relatively unconcerned about Loeb's blistering attacks. According to this argument, then, the two major influence
bases discussed so far are interrelated: perceived voter impact may
facilitate the operation of dislike of personal attack.

We have touched upon a fundamental condition for the direct
influence of a newspaper on candidates: the politicians must read
the paper or become informed in some other way about what positions the paper is taking. Why do politicians read the *Union Lead-*

88. Interview, not for attribution, 1968.

er? In part because of the belief that the newspaper shapes opinions and is an important element to take into consideration. William Dunfey says, concerning the *Union Leader:*

> It is *really* part of the fabric of how the political system works here, and anybody who thinks they're above it because they don't like the way he writes or the kind of paper that he has— they really don't get much above it. They stay out on the fringes of politics; they're not in the middle. . . . And there are probably a lot of people like the people in Hanover who say, "Oh hell, I don't read that paper." Well, this is pretty stupid. They don't read it, and they don't understand what is going on in the state. And when they come down to Manchester or to Concord for the education group or for the state convention or some kind of a meeting, they don't have any sense or relation to what the practical problems are of enlisting broad support for what they're involved in.[89]

Mrs. Sylvia Chaplain, a Democratic political activist and 1972 congressional candidate from the Manchester suburb of Bedford, reports:

> I can't think of anyone who's at all interested in the political scene and what's going on in community affairs who doesn't read it [the *Union Leader*]—hating themselves as they read it. I can't do without it. . . . I've got to know what the lines of thinking are because I'm involved in politics, and—you know, if you don't read it you don't know what he [Loeb] is trying to do or the lines he's trying to follow.[90]

Besides the feeling that Loeb is influential with New Hampshire citizens, the desire to be informed about state politics stimulates political activists to read the *Union Leader*. For the Manchester paper has a larger staff than other New Hampshire dailies and carries more extensive news coverage of politics, including a smattering of stories from throughout the state. From this point of view, control over political information by the *Union Leader* in-

89. Interview with William L. Dunfey, September 12, 1967.
90. Interview with Sylvia Chaplain, August 28, 1967.

duces politicians to read the paper and thus serves as a potential influence base for the paper.

David C. Hoeh—formerly of Hanover, manager of Senator Eugene McCarthy's 1968 presidential primary campaign, and 1968 congressional candidate himself—agrees that *Union Leader* influence is magnified by its widespread readership by politicians. But Hoeh disagrees that it is necessary for politically concerned citizens to read the paper to keep aware of Loeb's positions or to obtain political information:

> The impact of the *Union Leader* should be far less than it really is. But the problem is that the politicians read the *Union Leader*, and everyone who thinks that they should be versed in statewide politics in New Hampshire thinks they have to read the *Union Leader* and think they have to respond to the *Union Leader*. And they don't. . . . It's supposed to have the best statewide news coverage. Now I don't believe this, though I'm not saying that the other papers are that good. . . .[91]

Hoeh points out, though, that his own experiences have been confined largely to the Second Congressional District, in which the *Union Leader's* circulation is much lower than in the First District.[92] No other interviewed politician dismissed the value of reading the *Union Leader*.

The fact that candidates and their advisers read the *Union Leader* enables the Loeb press to help define political reality for politicians. This "cognitive political mapmaking" process includes the transmission and structuring of political information, including information about Loeb's statements. Continuous exposure to the *Union Leader* thus might exert a subtle influence on a candidate's image of state politics. Perhaps this mechanism is what David Hoeh has in mind when he says that New Hampshire politicians "think they have to respond to the *Union Leader*" and "are conditioned by it."[93]

91. Interview with David C. Hoeh, August 3, 1967.
92. According to 1966 circulation figures and 1966 population estimates, *Union Leader* circulation divided by population was 10.1 percent in the First District and 5.6 percent in the Second District.
93. Interview with David C. Hoeh, August 3, 1967.

In short, my analysis of the reasons for the *Union Leader's* influence on candidates' decisions leads to the following conclusions. One main influence base, the belief by political strategists that the *Union Leader* has a significant impact on the electorate, can be traced to two characteristics of the paper: its vigorous political advocacy and its circulation dominance. The second main influence base is the candidates' dislike of receiving Loeb's strong editorial attacks. The operation of these two factors is facilitated by the fact that candidates and their advisers do read the *Union Leader*. They pay attention to it because they think it influences voters and because it contains more extensive statewide news coverage than any other New Hampshire paper.

CHAPTER FOUR

The News Transmission Process

What kind of campaign news reaches the public? How do candidates and newspapermen determine the content of this news? In answering such questions I shall pay particular attention to the *Union Leader* but also discuss other papers in both New Hampshire and Vermont.

The Nature of Campaign News Coverage in New Hampshire

With small staffs and several campaigns to cover in an election year, New Hampshire daily newspapers rely heavily on candidates' press releases as a source of news. Most papers print these releases ("handouts") and also make use of wire-service stories, which themselves are based mainly on candidates' press releases. In addition, when a candidate campaigns in the area of a newspaper, a story is usually written about him by one of the paper's reporters. Finally, many newspapers write a "background" story on a major statewide candidate near the end of the campaign.

The reliance on candidates for the generation of campaign news is even more pronounced on the part of the weekly newspapers than the dailies. Whereas the weeklies vary widely in the amount of coverage they devote to politics, most of these papers print a story on a candidate only if he is in the area of the paper—and usually only if he pays a visit to the newspaper's office.

The amount of background or feature news available to the

evening dailies increased in 1962 when most of these papers joined
to form the State News Service. They jointly employ one reporter,
operating out of Concord. At present (1974) five of the evening
dailies belong to the State News Service. Despite this effort to
bolster the amount of background reporting, however, New Hampshire's newspapers continue to rely heavily on the candidates
themselves for campaign news.[1]

Most of the journalists I talked with are unhappy about reliance
on candidates' handouts. For example, Frank B. Merrick, former
State News Service reporter, complains:

> This is one real weak point of the New Hampshire press. . . . The
> newspapers are so small that they are unable to give full coverage
> to the major candidates even after the primary. As a result, the
> candidates tend to run their elections on handouts. . . . I try to
> overcome it. I try to spend a couple of days with each candidate
> and sit down and do an in-depth story on this candidate. But
> even so I can't hope to cover his positions on the issues in the
> story. . . . If you let a politician run it on handouts, he's in the
> driver's seat. He's determining what you're publishing.[2]

Indeed, a few newspapermen suggest that objective reporting must
place politicians' statements in a meaningful context. According to
this view, simply printing handouts without interpretive material
can be biased and misleading.

On the other hand, a defense of printing handouts is made by
George E. Connell, general manager of the *Union Leader*, which
like the other papers relies heavily on candidates' releases. Connell

1. The above generalizations on campaign news coverage by and large hold
true for Vermont as well as New Hampshire. However, a break with the traditional pattern was made in the coverage of the 1966 gubernatorial election in
Vermont. The Rutland *Herald* assigned one reporter to travel with each candidate during the last five weeks of the campaign. Three reporters were ro-
tated on a weekly basis, so that each spent time with both of the candidates.
The result was two stories every day, one on each of the candidates, the stories being printed on page one under a common headline. The Burlington *Free
Press* adopted a variation of this system of coverage during the campaign's
final three weeks. The *Herald* has continued this travel-with-the-candidate
approach in the years since 1966.

2. Interview with Frank B. Merrick, May 2, 1968.

views the publishing of politicians' statements verbatim, without rewriting, as allowing the candidates to present their views to the public in an undistorted manner.[3]

In short, New Hampshire newspaper coverage (as well as radio and television coverage) tends to act as a transmitter of messages generated by candidates, with little alteration of the content of these messages. The media can thus be viewed as relatively passive instruments of communication which must be "used" by candidates to reach the voters. A candidate might enhance or diminish the favorability of his news coverage by communicating skillfully or poorly with the press. Nevertheless, candidates are dependent on the media in the first place for the inclusion of their statements in the news. Moreover, newspaper personnel determine the degree of prominence given to these messages in the news columns. And of course the important operation of headline writing is out of the candidate's control. Thus even if newspapers are relatively passive instruments of communication, they can still do much to determine the form in which candidates' messages reach the public.

Of crucial importance in determining what citizens read about a campaign are journalists' basic conceptions of newsworthiness: What kinds of matters do journalists consider to be news? With regard to the *Union Leader*, an answer to this question might run as follows. Candidates' statements are newsworthy (especially the positions of candidates supported by the *Union Leader*); conversely, in-depth background information about social or political conditions is not newsworthy. More specifically, easily dramatized, sensational, emotional statements are newsworthy—for example, personal attacks on opponents or other individuals (even newspaper publishers). Also, issues considered important by the *Union Leader* (like state taxes) are newsworthy. The list could be extended.

The *Union Leader's* definition of news value is important in New Hampshire because it influences other newspapers' perceptions of what is news, at least with respect to specific stories. This statement should be read as a hypothesis rather than a firm conclusion, since I have little supporting evidence; however, I find statements by three Concord *Monitor* staff members to be significant.

3. Interview with George E. Connell, November 3, 1967.

Monitor editor and assistant publisher Thomas W. Gerber asserts that William Loeb is able to set the topic and tone of public debate in New Hampshire and remarks, "We respond to the issues that he establishes—the tax issue, for instance." Gerber observes that his paper frequently enters a Loeb-initiated story by printing politicians' responses to positions taken by the *Union Leader* publisher.[4] Political editor and reporter Rod Paul says he tries not to react to Loeb's paper but that he is not always successful. Paul states that the wire services (especially important as a source for radio news) routinely write "reaction" stories by politicians commenting on material appearing in the *Union Leader*.[5] And general manager George W. Wilson tells me he concluded his own news judgment was being unduly shaped by the *Union Leader*, so he stopped reading the paper for a period of several months.[6] *Union Leader* influence on the news of other media certainly merits more extensive investigation than I have given it.

It has become common for New Hampshire candidates and journalists to question the news judgments made by editors deciding which handouts to print and how much "play" to give them. The *Union Leader* has been severely criticized for giving unfair advantage in news coverage to Loeb-supported candidates, regardless of professional considerations of newsworthiness. For example, the Concord *Monitor's* Thomas Gerber says about handouts: "We try to look at 'em on an objective basis with a view to the interests of the people among whom we circulate. . . . If Meldrim Thomson announces the appointment of a town chairman in Colebrook, it's not going to have any interest locally. Yet Loeb will carry that; and we won't."[7] (See the following chapter for data on news coverage relevant to this criticism of the *Union Leader*.)

On the other hand, the Loeb press has accused other papers of hiding behind a "local interest" conception of newsworthiness as an excuse to deny coverage to candidates opposed by those papers. Near the end of the 1970 Republican gubernatorial primary, Loeb

4. Interview with Thomas W. Gerber, August 25, 1972.
5. Interview with Rod Paul, August 25, 1972.
6. Conversation with George W. Wilson, July 26, 1972.
7. Interview with Thomas W. Gerber, August 25, 1972.

made this complaint about the coverage given *Union-Leader*-backed Meldrim Thomson, Jr.:

> With the exception of this newspaper and a few other pro-Thomson papers, the vast majority of the bleeding-heart, left-wing, sales-and-income-tax minded newspapers in the state have downgraded or ignored Thomson's campaign almost completely and kept from their readers the news of what he has been saying. In many other cases they have poured forth a torrent of venomous lies against Thomson, misrepresenting his positions and shamelessly lying about him.[8]

The *Union Leader* resounded with similar complaints in 1972 and at one point printed news coverage data purporting to demonstrate that "these journalistic prostitutes have shown themselves to be INCAPABLE of giving anything approaching FAIR news coverage to the candidates they oppose."[9] Criticism of unfairness in news judgments certainly has not been confined to opponents of the *Union Leader*.

The Role of Newspapers in Issue Definition: The Tax Issue

The amount of news coverage for a candidate and the placement of those stories are salient concerns of candidates. Another important aspect of news coverage is the content of stories and headlines written by reporters and editors. In New Hampshire, headline content is especially significant, since story content consists mainly of candidates' press releases. And of course headlines are particularly important for the many readers who skim them and do not bother to read the stories

This section examines the role of newspapers in defining or labeling a complex issue through the writing of headlines and news stories. Our "case study" issue is taxes, which, as noted in Chapter

8. "Happy Holiday BUT—Don't Forget Sept. 8!" *Union Leader* (September 5, 1970), p. 1.
9. "Whatever Became of Fair Play?" *Union Leader* (October 24, 1972).

3, has been the dominant issue in New Hampshire gubernatorial campaigns for many years. The amount of news coverage and campaign discussion devoted to taxes is matched by the great importance of this issue for the operation of state government and for New Hampshire citizens in general.

The New Hampshire revenue structure rests heavily on the local property tax. The state government receives funds mainly from horse racing, liquor sales, a business profits tax, and a rooms-and-meals tax. But alone among the fifty states, New Hampshire has never had a general sales or income tax—in political parlance a broad-base tax.

Tax-change advocates stress the desirability of adopting such a tax in order to relieve pressure on the regressive local property tax. Moreover, such individuals argue for new state expenditures that could be financed by additional revenues. These aspects of the problem are played down by supporters of the status quo, who emphasize the undesirability of all new taxes, and the opposing strategies are mirrored in the choice of terminology: advocates of change speak of the "tax reform issue," while their opponents refer to the "sales tax issue," "income tax issue," or "broad-base tax issue." The mere selection of terminology to define the issue involves a focusing of attention on some aspects of the problem at the expense of others and thus helps to structure the issue in such a way that one side is aided while the other side is hampered. One group would like to debate the merits of new state expenditures (or tax reform), while the other group wants to discuss whether a new tax is desirable per se. Underlying this strategic reasoning is the assumption that voters are more favorably disposed toward new expenditures or the elimination of existing taxes than toward additional taxes.

In a situation in which labeling an issue involves a choice between loaded terms, one might expect some candidates to feel unhappy with at least part of the media reporting and headline writing. This expectation is correct. The consensus among the candidates is that news coverage stresses the sales or income-tax aspect of the issue, and the advocates of the additional tax feel that this emphasis is misplaced.

The first major candidate to call openly for tax revision that
would include the addition of a general sales or income tax was
Zandy Taft, who was defeated for the Republican gubernatorial
nomination in 1966. In order to consolidate hard-core support
early in the campaign, Taft felt that he had to indicate clearly his
support of a broad-base tax. Thus he urged the adoption of a sales
tax or an income tax, or a combination of the two, the precise
formula to be determined by the Legislature. Then, having taken
his stand, Taft attempted to stress aspects other than the necessity
of new taxes. Taft's program emphasized the need for increased
state expenditures in several areas, especially education and health
and welfare. Moreover, he felt that revision of the present tax
structure was desirable, including the lowering of local property
taxes. He says: "These things built up to the basic premise that we
need some form of broad-base tax in order to abolish certain taxes
and to rely on the funds that were needed both at the state level
and to filter back to the local level to relieve the property tax. . . .
Essentially I am talking needs [in his standard speech], and it is
only in the end that I say we need tax reform."[10]

Taft wanted the public debate to focus on state expenditure
needs rather than on taxes. Indeed, he hoped to keep the discussion off the subject of tax *reform*, in favor of substantive *needs*.
What he wanted to avoid most of all was attention to the question
of additional taxes. His opponents, however, stressed the sales-tax
aspect of the issue.

Taft thinks that the news coverage activities of the media (not
just the *Union Leader*) placed emphasis on the wrong part of the
issue:

But unfortunately the headline writers kept saying, "Taft Advocates Sales Tax," "Taft Advocates Income Tax." . . . I think
it's an unfortunate thing, but the average person will scan headlines. This is why I say that headlines hurt me on the basis of
saying, "Taft Advocates Broad-Base Tax" or "Taft Advocates
Tax Reform." It should have been "Taft Advocates Help for
Education," "Taft Advocates Help for Mental Health," and so

10. Interview with Alexander M. Taft, July 25, 1967.

on. They should have been underplaying the tax program. People
kept saying "Taft Wants Taxes," and they wouldn't read into
why he wanted taxes.[11]

Taft feels that his message came across better on radio and television newscasts than in newspapers. A person reading just headlines would miss Taft's statement of spending needs, but this
message was usually included in the summary by the electronic
media: "Although it was condensed, it still was better at making
the point you wanted to get across."[12]

More recent advocates of tax reform have also resented press
coverage of the tax issue, especially the *Union Leader* coverage. In
his 1970 reelection campaign, Governor Walter Peterson firmly
opposed the adoption of a broad-base tax. Peterson changed his
mind, however, and made the following statement in his January
1971 inaugural address to the Legislature:

> We must—you and I—pay for our past sin: that of not opening
> up to cool-headed public debate the question of broad-base
> taxes. But we must have the courage to withstand the destructive
> powers of the Loeb press and tell the public what it does not
> seem to understand: that our tax structure is, and always has
> been, a reflection of the wishes of the well-to-do. We must ac-
> knowledge that income taxes, based on ability to pay, need not
> hit the low wage earner, and could provide significant relief for
> the elderly and for the hard-pressed property taxpayer.[13]

However, the Legislature rejected several tax reform proposals.
Running in the 1972 Republican gubernatorial primary, Peterson
stressed the need for tax reform and especially emphasized the
desirability of cutting property taxes. However, he is not satisfied
with *Union Leader* coverage of his position:

> If for example you are trying to drastically cut the property
> tax—as we were—by eliminating that portion of the property

11. Ibid.
12. Ibid.
13. Quoted in "Peterson Switches Tax Stand in Inaugural Address," *Union
Leader* (January 8, 1971), p. 5.

tax that goes for education and pick it up with an income tax based on a person's ability to pay, for more than half the people of the state it represents a tax cut. Yet this is not the way it's presented to the public [by the *Union Leader*]. The way it's presented to the public is that these are just additional taxes to be piled on top of what you're paying now. . . . So that you get people who would not vote against you otherwise, who on that one issue alone . . . vote against the person who is trying to fight for reform. Well, the result of this is higher property taxes and a higher tax burden for the low and moderate income person. . . . There's no effort made, you see, to educate the people that this is actually what happens. So in a sense it's a way to keep people down and keep the less affluent sector of the populace paying a disproportionate share of the tax burden while at the same time loudly trumpeting that you're helping them.[14]

Another 1972 candidate, Democratic gubernatorial primary aspirant Robert E. Raiche, advocated tax reform that included the addition of a state income tax and the drastic reduction of property taxes. Raiche feels that his position was difficult to communicate through the mass media: "It's an educational process. It's easier to say 'Anti-tax, period'—it requires no explanation—than it is to say 'Yes a tax, and tax reform' and then explain it."[15]

Asked whether his newspapers do not distort the messages of tax-reform candidates like Peterson and Raiche, William Loeb responds: "We claim, and I think our readers agree with us, that there is no such animal as a replacement of a tax by another tax—that if you don't end up with two new taxes, you end up at least with a tax and a half. So we will not help Mr. Peterson and Mr. Raiche in creating that delusion on the part of the public."[16]

Beyond defining the issue as "new taxes" rather than "tax reform" or "new expenditures," the *Union Leader* has tried to refine it further, to the benefit of opponents of tax change, by insisting that gubernatorial candidates pledge to *veto* a broad-base tax measure in return for Loeb support.

14. Interview with Walter Peterson, December 8, 1972.
15. Interview with Robert E. Raiche, October 13, 1972.
16. Interview with William Loeb, March 2, 1973.

The 1970 gubernatorial general election offers an example of the
veto-pledge tactic applied to news coverage of Governor Peterson,
who at that time still opposed broad-base taxes. A September 22nd
front-page news story begins: "Gov. Walter Peterson said yesterday
that he 'will not propose' either a sales or personal income tax to
the 1971 Legislature. He also told a State House press conference
yesterday morning he 'will not advocate' either of these broad-
base taxes. However, the governor once again avoided saying he
would veto either of the taxes if the Legislature should pass one."
The story is headlined "Peterson Avoids Tax Veto Stand."[17]
Reinforcing this message two days later, William Loeb asserts in
his front-page editorial, "Walter, We've Heard That Song Before":
"There you have the simple, one overriding issue of this campaign
for governor of New Hampshire. Governor Peterson refused to say
whather he would veto a sales or income tax. Roger Crowley, the
Democratic candidate, has come out flatly and said he will veto a
sales or income tax."[18]

The veto-promise question has been resented by several candidates—even those opposing broad-base taxes—who have considered
this pledge to be an unjustified limitation on a governor's freedom
of maneuver once he takes office. The veto pledge has frequently
been labeled "phony," for example by 1958 and 1960 Democratic
gubernatorial nominee Bernard L. Boutin, who calls the topic "this
phony issue put out by the Manchester *Union Leader*."[19] However,
a more recent candidate who took the pledge, 1968 Democratic
nominee Emile R. Bussiere, defends the veto promise as a legitimate
means of clarifying the tax issue for the voters:

For a few campaigns, I think around '58 and '60, I personally
thought that the pledge to veto situation was an unwarranted
issue. But as the years went on, through John King's campaigns
—and certainly when John King was going to get out of office in
'68—I felt that the issue was a very live issue, one that warranted

17. "Peterson Avoids Tax Veto Stand," *Union Leader* (September 22,
1970), p. 1.
18. "Walter, We've Heard That Song Before," *Union Leader* (September
24, 1970), p. 1.
19. Interview with Bernard L. Boutin, April 20, 1968.

primary attention. . . . I don't think there's any question that
there was an element in the political circles in New Hampshire—
they were partly Democrats and partly Republicans—that were
hell-bent on having an income tax or a sales tax in the coming
two-year period. . . . In my way of thinking it was always as if
you were conducting a referendum. If you could get that issue
that clearly laid in front of the electorate and identify one party
with it and one party on the other side of it, then in effect
you're electing a governor by referendum on that issue.[20]

Vermont offers some comparisons with New Hampshire on the
definition of the tax issue. In the mid-1960's Vermont had a
personal income tax but not a general sales tax. Richard A.
Snelling, the 1966 Republican gubernatorial nominee, ran on a tax
reform program which included the application of a sales tax. Like
Zandy Taft and similar candidates in New Hampshire, Snelling
stressed the benefits of additional tax revenue: increased state
expenditures for some services and the proposed reduction of income and property taxes.[21] On the other hand, his primary and
general election opponents concentrated on the undesirability of
a sales tax.

Snelling thinks that the content of news stories in the campaign
tended to simplify his tax program in an unfavorable manner.
Although most of the reporters tried hard to be fair, he believes,
almost all of them personally opposed the tax.[22] Snelling feels that
in some cases—particularly the wire service reporters—personal
opinion was reflected in the writing of news stories: "I do know
that their terminology tended, no matter how much I tried to do

20. Interview with Emile R. Bussiere, August 23, 1972.

21. An excerpt from a Burlington *Free Press* editorial exemplifies the strategy of defining the issue as "tax reform" rather than "sales tax": "As we have
pointed out many times, the sales tax is not the central issue. The major question is one of tax reform—which we believe is incapable of achievement without the adoption of a sales tax in concurrence with the reduction of income
and property taxes. Hopefully, no vote-seeking politician will try to muddy
the question again by raising the red flag of sales taxation" ("The Republican
Stand on Taxation," *Free Press*, September 23, 1966).

22. One reporter confides, "There's probably no doubt that every member
of the [State House] newsroom voted for Hoff"(interview with Steve Terry
of the Rutland *Herald*, November 28, 1967).

otherwise, to emphasize the sales tax rather than its purposes. For example, many of them, including the Associated Press, frequently would use my name followed by the phrase 'an advocate of the retail sales tax,' which was I thought an unfair oversimplification of the advocacy of an overall tax reform plan."[23] Snelling includes the two main political reporters of the Burlington *Free Press* in this indictment. Although the paper strongly supported him editorially, its reporters were favorable to Governor Philip H. Hoff. Snelling feels that he was able to get his message across to the voters more accurately through paid advertising than through news coverage by the press.

Like Taft, Snelling complains about the simplification in newspaper headlines:

If you make a half-an-hour talk in which you implore people to recognize the alternatives with respect to taxation and one of your eight conclusions is that you can't energize this whole formula without enacting a sales tax, and the headline in the newspaper says, "Snelling Makes Another Sales Tax Bid"—I'm suggesting to you that my experience in conversations with the people over and over again is that a substantial number of people read only the headlines and that what comes through is not the specifics.[24]

Snelling adds: "Modern media put a premium—a tremendous and to me a very dangerous premium—on whoever holds a position which may be most favorably summed up in a headline."[25] He lost the general election to Hoff.

In 1964 Robert S. Babcock ran unsuccessfully for the Republican gubernatorial nomination in Vermont and as his major issue advocated tax reform, including the addition of a sales tax. Babcock's strategy on the issue was similar to that of Snelling. Babcock also was not satisfied with the news coverage of the issue; he emphasizes the difficulty of reporting satisfactorily such a complicated matter:

23. Interview with Richard A. Snelling, November 20, 1967.
24. Ibid.
25. Ibid.

Q. Were you satisfied with the kind of coverage that the media gave the issue? Or gave your stand on the issue?

A. No, you never were, I never was satisfied. And it was understandable. It was always maddening, but it was understandable. Because involved in this sales tax was a reduction in the income tax, an abolition of the personal property tax, and a complete change in the poll tax. This is awful hard to explain in a speech; it's even harder to condense into a news article. And so the news articles almost always hit upon the sales tax, not the other aspects of it.[26]

Not surprisingly, the anti-sales-tax candidates are fairly satisfied with the way the issue was reported and regard the news coverage as having been straightforward. They feel that the addition of the new tax is the most important aspect of the issue and deserves to be emphasized. As in New Hampshire, the Vermont sales tax opponents criticize labeling the new tax proposals "tax reform." Like the statement by William Loeb quoted above, these politicians attack the contention that a sales tax would lower property taxes. For example, Babcock's victorious primary opponent, Ralph A. Foote, states: "I did get squarely to the question of it as a reform tax, as using it as bait to lessen some of our local taxes. It wouldn't accomplish this anyway. The history of state government doesn't go this way. You don't use new tax money, unfortunately, to reduce other taxes even though you may set out to do that in the first instance. You use new tax money to pay for new programs that all the pork barrel boys want to get involved with. And this was my stress, this is what I believe. And I think the public believes me."[27]

Thus the advocates of tax change want certain aspects of this complicated issue to be stressed, while their opponents feel that attention should be focused on other elements. If the press emphasizes one side or the other in news coverage, somebody is bound to be dissatisfied. The job of the newspaperman in this situation is not easy.

If the sales or income tax part of the issue is given the greatest

26. Interview with Robert S. Babcock, November 29, 1967.
27. Interview with Ralph A. Foote, January 19, 1968.

prominence, why is this the case? It could be argued that the new tax is the most dramatic change from the status quo in tax reform proposals and hence is most newsworthy. Moreover, a single additional tax is more easily understood than multiple changes in other taxes or changes in several areas of state expenditures. In addition, editors and reporters probably tend to play up the side of the argument which agrees most closely with their own attitudes. Conscious and blatant advocacy by newspapers, however, is less evident in Vermont than in New Hampshire.

The four Vermont reporters I talked to agree with the candidates that the sales tax aspect of the issue became dominant in the 1964 and 1966 campaigns. These men also realize the difficulty of reporting the issue objectively, but they feel that emphasis on the sales tax was not unfair. Concerning the tax issue in the Hoff-Snelling contest, Vic Maerki of the Burlington *Free Press* observes:

> All media tend to simplify, I hope not always to oversimplify. They have to simplify. . . . I've known Dick Snelling for a long time. He's a complicated guy who qualifies almost everything he says—as most intelligent people do, I think, on complex issues. . . . The point is that it was a sales tax. A reporter's job is to communicate, not to make a candidate happy. And he called it a lot of things, but it *was* a sales tax.[28]

The content of stories during the campaign was a frequently discussed subject between Snelling and reporters. Steve Terry, formerly a Rutland *Herald* reporter, says of the Republican candidate: "He'd say, 'Now, I don't want a sales tax; I want tax reform and tax relief.' . . . This was the basic issue, and he kept arguing about it with us." [29] The *Herald* reporters claim that they "leaned over backwards" to be fair to Snelling, particularly since their paper opposed him editorially. These newspapermen say that in stories they tried to explain Snelling's tax plan the way he wanted it

28. Interview with Vic Maerki, December 13, 1967.
29. From a taped discussion of the 1966 gubernatorial campaign by Rutland *Herald* reporters John Mahoney, Tony Marro, and Steve Terry (February 16, 1967). The tape was made available through the courtesy of Charles T. Morrissey, director of the Vermont Historical Society.

explained. But the issue was complicated; and headlines, which are not written by the reporters, are important in transmitting a candidate's message to the readers.

In summary, the observations of the interviewed politicians and reporters in New Hampshire and Vermont have called attention to the role of news coverage in focusing attention on certain facets of a complex issue at the expense of other aspects. As part of this process, complex messages of candidates are digested into a small space. This condensation is a necessary function of simplifying material into the form that reaches the audience. Even if newspaper personnel try to perform this activity in an unbiased manner, certain facets of an issue or a position on an issue are likely to receive greater emphasis than others, and some participants gain a corresponding advantage. In news stories and headlines even the choice of terminology to label controversies (e.g., is it the "sales tax issue" or "tax reform issue"?) results in benefits to one side of the argument. At least this is the belief of the participants. The opinion is reflected in choice of strategies; each side uses what it feels is a favorable label or definition of the issue.

In Chapter 3 I observed that by defining the tax issue in a certain way, newspapers can help to initiate issues by influencing candidates' strategic calculations. I noted that by defining the issue as whether or not a gubernatorial candidate promises to veto a tax bill if elected, the *Union Leader* has made it profitable for some candidates to introduce the subject of taxes into the campaign discussion. In this way issue definition by newspapers may sometimes play a part in the process of issue initiation.

Perhaps the most significant aspect of the issue-definition process is what is *not* defined as news, or *not* discussed in a campaign. Several New Hampshire interviewees complain that the emphasis given taxes detracts from such substantive problems as education, housing, and health care. Speaking in 1967, a member of Governor King's staff argues: "You're talking about it backwards. What you should be doing is talking about positive things; and if you need a sales tax to pay for better education, this is something which will come later when you get to the Legislature. But instead of that, the thing gets turned around backwards and the sales tax becomes a major campaign issue. . . . The real problems of the state seldom really get gone into in a campaign."[30] More recently, Robert Raiche observes: "The tax question clouds the real issues; it always has. It clouds the real social issues facing the state."[31]

Candidates' Techniques for Obtaining Good Coverage

There exists a wide range among New Hampshire and Vermont statewide candidates in the degree to which they perform their media-related activities on the basis of systematic strategic calculations. Secondly, most candidates probably have not calculated strategically with respect to press relations.

The evidence for these assertions is not solid but is based on my subjective impressions of the candidates' interview responses. These generalizations were made, however, by several observers close to the political scene. For example, in 1968 Concord *Monitor* reporter Jack Hubbard said it was his impression that compared with politicians in other states where he had worked (including California and Maine), New Hampshire candidates do not think in terms of using the media as communications instruments to their own advantage.[32]

If candidates in New Hampshire and Vermont have been comparatively unconcerned about their methods of communicating through the media, part of the explanation may be the strong tradition of personal campaigning in the two states—getting out and meeting the voters face-to-face. A number of interviewees feel that the electorate expects to meet the candidates in person. Perhaps many politicians have concentrated their time and effort to reach the voters in this way rather than through the news columns. It appears that the candidates who have devoted the most attention to communicating through the media have been younger politicians, relative newcomers, who are probably less rooted in the traditions of their state and more open to innovations. Another possible

30. Interview, not for attribution, September 6, 1967.
31. Interview with Robert E. Raiche, October 13, 1972.
32. Interview with Jack Hubbard, May 2, 1968.

explanation for the degree of strategic sophistication of different candidates is provided by several interviewees who express the opinion that more advanced public relations techniques (including advertising innovations) were first used by Democratic candidates in the late 1950's. Perhaps the "out" party in a relatively one-party system is more open to new strategies and tactics than the incumbent party, which may be content to rely on methods which have worked in the past.

The degree of sophistication in campaign communications has clearly increased in recent years. Especially for advertising, major statewide candidates in New Hampshire are making greater use of campaign consultants and public relations firms. Virtually unknown fifteen years ago, systematic polling is now common. Whatever may have been the case in the recent past, modern campaign techniques have arrived in New Hampshire and Vermont. At the same time, the tradition of meeting the voters in person remains strong.

Two examples of candidates whose strategies have systematically taken account of the media are 1966 Republican gubernatorial candidates Richard Snelling (Vermont) and William Johnson (New Hampshire). Both Snelling and Johnson were very concerned about communicating through the media (a Vermont reporter says that when Snelling ran for lieutenant governor in 1964, he regularly measured the number of column-inches of coverage he received in different papers).[33] Basic to the strategic thinking of both Snelling and Johnson was the assumption that many more voters could be reached through newspapers than through personal contact. Both men attached high strategic priority to the goal of obtaining extensive and prominent news coverage.

A main part of both Snelling's and Johnson's campaign strategy was based on the assumption that a candidate receives more prominent coverage if he campaigns in the area of a newspaper or radio station than if he just mails out a press release. In addition to having his statement printed, he might have his picture taken or be interviewed. Johnson was particularly aware of coverage in weekly newspapers, many of which do not print a story about a candidate unless he is physically present in the paper's readership area.

33. Interview with John Mahoney of the Rutland *Herald*, November 28, 1967.

These considerations led to the conclusion that the candidate should maximize his contact with local newspapers and radio stations. Primarily for this purpose, Snelling and Johnson both traveled very extensively in a campaign bus. The schedule entailed much traveling because of the number of media in each state and the lack of one mass medium reaching all the voters. Here is a response by Snelling:

Q. You covered a great deal of territory criss-crossing the state. Was this strategy focused in part on the media? For example, the attempt to get into as many local newspaper areas as possible?

A. Yes. This whole schedule was prepared with the specific belief that newspapers will be more easily induced to print what you say if you said it in their territory. And so I had a schedule which was rather complicated. . . . The thought was to be in the area of every newspaper at least once a week, and we did that. And at the same time we did many other things; we would stop in for chats with the radio disc jockeys, and so on. We had every medium in the state arranged in a "how can we see them most often" basis. And the schedule was arranged exactly with that in mind.[34]

Johnson, whose strategic calculations were similar, says: "What I came to recognize was the fact that if you're going to make news in Portsmouth, you gotta be in Portsmouth. And so we developed the idea of a fast-moving campaign—keep going, always on the move, to be in as many places as possible. So that you were in the town, made a statement in the city, and the editor could see you and could look you in the eyeball and you gave him a news release which you purported was made in his town. . . . A statement made today in Exeter now became Exeter news. And you were outside the editor's office with your campaign bus; that was news. So we'd move, move, constantly on the move."[35] Johnson felt he had to make news in the many local newspapers partly because of the communications advantage General Thyng enjoyed in the *Union Leader*.

34. Interview with Richard A. Snelling, January 19, 1968.
35. Interview with William R. Johnson, September 16, 1967.

Snelling and Johnson are both satisfied with their travel-to-the-media strategy; they think that they got better coverage than if they had utilized press releases in the more conventional manner. This strategy had at least one drawback, however: the constant traveling was physically demanding. Regarding his continual motion strategy, Snelling says: "It exhausted me, frankly, which I've never said to anybody. I was pretty well shot, and I don't get shot very easily. . . . It made a physical toll on a candidate which may begin to make him less sharp in his visibility."[36] Johnson also reports that his campaign schedule was physically tiring. He feels that this weariness might facilitate a candidate's making a major blunder, though Johnson says that he avoided this pitfall.[37] Carried to the lengths of Snelling and Johnson, the continual motion strategy might be difficult if not impossible for a candidate older or less vigorous than these two men (in 1966 Snelling was 39, Johnson, 35).

If the importance of a strategic decision is measured by the amount of time and energy expended in implementing that decision, considerations of making news were important for the campaign strategies of both Snelling and Johnson. In Chapter 3 I discussed strategies in the sense of decisions about the *content* of appeals to be made in a campaign. The present perspective views strategies as decisions about the *method* through which such appeals are to be communicated.

For many candidates the *Union Leader* has had an impact not only on "content" strategies, but also on "method" strategies. The structure of Johnson's campaign can be seen as an attempt to develop and utilize communications channels other than the *Union Leader*. An even better example is Senator McIntyre, who regularly times his press releases for the deadlines of the afternoon dailies and who has systematically constructed good working relationships with the non-*Union Leader* media. Well before the start of his 1972 campaign McIntyre made a series of personal visits to many newspapers (including weeklies and "shoppers") and released "exclusive" stories to individual papers. McIntyre continued these

36. Interview with Richard A. Snelling, January 19, 1968.
37. Interview with William R. Johnson, May 1, 1968.

efforts during the campaign itself. One of his top assistants states: "What we were trying to do was to build communication systems other than the *Union Leader*. It was a clear attempt to countervail it. . . . This was a heavy expenditure of the Senator's personal time—in close, detailed, precise, exclusive, personalized press relations."[38] Reflecting on the campaign, this man considers these efforts to have been very successful. One measure of the *Union Leader's* importance is the amount of hard work some of the paper's opponents have undertaken in attempts to counteract the dominance of the Loeb press.

One relatively recent innovation employed by McIntyre and some other candidates has been the use of "beepers" or "actualities" for radio communication. This technique involves renting a telephone WATS line, which is used to transmit recorded statements directly to radio stations. It is very convenient for a station to broadcast such a message on a news program.

With an eye on future news coverage and editorials, candidates generally pay attention to establishing and maintaining good personal relations with editors and reporters. However, such efforts may backfire. Former McIntyre press aide John Barker, who previously was a Portsmouth *Herald* reporter, observes: "As soon as you start cuddling up to some editor, he's going to rebel because they are independent and they like to think they are independent; even the wire people, they're independent. They aren't for you and you aren't for them. What you want to do is give them good service and you want to give them fast service, effective service. And what will happen in practice is if you do it this way you will get your message across."[39] And Vic Maerki of the Burlington *Free Press* remarks:

> The reporters here face a dilemma like they do in Washington and any place else. Very often a good, close personal relationship results in good stories for the reporter who has that relationship. On the other hand, you have to concern yourself with what price you pay for that kind of relationship. . . . The reporters that I know vary from one extreme to the other—some who cul-

38. Interview, not for attribution, November 17, 1972.
39. Interview with John Barker, September 25, 1967.

tivate these friendships in hopes of cultivating a big story and others who deliberately keep their distance. I subscribe to the latter. I think it's a good idea to keep at arm's length.[40]

Thus, from the perspective of a candidate attempting to obtain good coverage, close personal relations are likely to be more successful with some journalists than with others.

Candidates have tried to go beyond the pattern of making statements and distributing press releases. Benjamin Collins, a top aide of Governor Hoff, says in 1967: "We probably rely less than any candidate on press releases, handouts. . . . I suppose part of the reason is that I was a reporter for a while. Bill Kearns, who is also close to the Governor, was also a reporter. And quite a few of the guys in the administration have a press background. My own experience was every time I got a political handout, I was ready to throw it away, you know. . . . So my approach is to have him make news, do something that is newsworthy, rather than hand out a lot of pap."[41] Collins adds that it is much easier for an incumbent than a challenger to "make news" through actions instead of press releases alone.

Although candidates' releases remain the prime source of campaign news, most of the journalists I interviewed think that politicians are not especially skillful at writing the content of their statements so as to appeal to newspapers. Thomas Gerber suspects that the *Union Leader* has something to do with the poor news judgment of candidates. When I asked Gerber in his 1972 interview whether gubernatorial and senatorial candidates have much room for improvement in the art of making news, he replied:

Oh yeah, my God, they don't have the foggiest notion of how to go about it; they really don't. They don't know what news is; I'm not necessarily saying they should, but they ought to have people around them who do. They don't know what it is to create news, because the criterion of judgment is warped by Loeb printing everything they do. So they think that 'All I've gotta do is make a statement and I'll end up on page one.'[42]

40. Interview with Vic Maerki, December 13, 1967.
41. Interview with Benjamin Collins, November 28, 1967.
42. Interview with Thomas W. Gerber, August 25, 1972.

Despite such general complaints, many interviewed journalists stated that a few candidates are proficient at making news.

A main criticism by newspapermen is that candidates do not stress matters of local interest in their handouts. Several 1967 remarks by Lebanon *Valley News* personnel are illustrative. Managing editor Stephen Taylor says, "Candidates don't know how to come in here and say something that appeals to an editor here, about this local area." Taylor adds that if a candidate discusses a local matter like the regional airport, "this is great, it makes good copy. If he comes in and he talks about wheat exports or shoe imports or something that doesn't have much impact around here, my reaction—I know I shouldn't do it—but my reaction is well, it's inside page stuff."[43] And assistant publisher Marvin Midgette reports, "Usually what we do frankly is look through the releases first and see if there is a local angle."[44]

For all aspects of press relations, it is useful for a candidate to have someone with newspaper experience on his staff. It is much easier for an incumbent governor or senator to attract such a person by offering him a salaried position. The challenger, on the other hand, may have difficulty locating a top-notch journalist who is willing to work during the relatively short period of a campaign. It is no accident that the candidates whose press work was most frequently praised by interviewed newspapermen were incumbents. A good example is former Vermont Governor Hoff, whose top three aides were journalists. In 1967 Burlington *Free Press* editor Gordon Mills remarked that Hoff's staff members "know newspapering and know what newspapers consider to be news."[45]

43. Interview with Stephen Taylor, September 20, 1967.
44. Interview with Marvin Midgette, November 1, 1967.
45. Interview with Gordon Mills, December 19, 1967.

CHAPTER FIVE

The Effect of the *Union Leader* on the Electorate

I have argued that a vital base of influence for the Loeb press is the belief by politicians that it has a significant impact on the electorate, and this belief may in turn be shaped by whether the paper actually does exert such influence.

Newspapers and radio or television stations may be important as transmitters of influential messages from candidates, but it would be a mistake to view them as passive channels for politicians attempting to persuade an audience. The media become actively involved by selecting which messages to transmit and which to ignore. Moreover, through their editorials newspapers generate their own messages.

Two kinds of influence are exerted by mass media content. The first is a change in direction of an opinion: for example, a potential voter becomes either more or less favorable toward a candidate. A sufficiently great change of direction results in *conversion*: the voter who once favored candidate X now intends to vote for his opponent, candidate Y. "Conversion" could also denote a switch from a neutral or undecided posture.

The second kind of effect is a change in the intensity with which an opinion is held. A person might definitely favor candidate X over candidate Y, but not strongly. Upon reading more information about candidate X, however, the citizen becomes a more intense partisan. Whereas he might not have intended to vote before, now he will go to the polls—and maybe even actively try to convince others of candidate X's virtues. Thus a sufficient change in intensity of an opinion leads to the *activation* of the opinion hold-er. Just as conversion is a qualitative change resulting from a quantitative change in direction of an opinion, activation is a qualitative change resulting from a quantitative change in intensity.

Although social scientists have not extensively researched the impact of the mass media on the electorate, the available evidence gives us reason to be skeptical about the ability of political communication to convert opinions. For example, in their classic Erie County panel study of the 1940 presidential campaign, Paul F. Lazarsfeld and associates found that only 8 percent of the sample finally decided to vote for a party other than their original choice in May. During the campaign the vote intentions of only 12 percent of the sample wavered between parties. The main effect of the barrage of political communication was to crystallize earlier intentions or predispositions.[1] Two studies indicate that fewer than 10 percent of voters switched candidate preference as a result of the 1960 Kennedy-Nixon television debates.[2] On the level of state politics, a survey of reactions to a telethon in the 1958 California gubernatorial campaign suggests that almost no conversions took place as a result of the broadcast.[3] And John E. Mueller found no evidence that Los Angeles area newspapers influenced voters in a series of 1964 referendum propositions.[4]

Why is conversion a rare phenomenon? First, messages aimed at persuasion in public affairs often do not reach a sizable number of citizens. Many people do not seek out political information; for the vast majority of citizens, political matters have a low saliency and are overshadowed by personal and family concerns.[5] Many

1. Paul F. Lazarsfeld, Bernard Berelson, and Hazel Gaudet, *The People's Choice* (New York: Columbia University Press, 1948), pp. 65–66.

2. Paul J. Deutschmann, "Viewing, Conversion, and Voting Intentions," in Sidney Kraus, ed., *The Great Debates* (Bloomington: Indiana University Press, 1962), pp. 232–252. Kurt Lang and Gladys Engel Lang, "Ordeal by Debate: Viewer Reactions," *Public Opinion Quarterly*, 25 (1961), 277–288. Deutschmann's study examines viewer reactions before and after the first debate only, while the Langs' project encompasses all four debates.

3. Wilbur Schramm and Richard F. Carter, "Effectiveness of a Political Telethon," *Public Opinion Quarterly*, 23 (1959), 121–127.

4. John E. Mueller, "Voting on the Propositions: Ballot Patterns and Historical Trends in California," *American Political Science Review*, 63 (1969), 1197–1212.

5. For example, see Robert S. Erikson and Norman R. Luttbeg, *American*

individuals do not read a newspaper primarily to inform themselves about public affairs but rather for such purposes as assistance in daily living or relaxation.[6] Accordingly, numerous surveys
have demonstrated a low level of political information on the part
of Americans.[7] Reflecting the prevailing skepticism toward the
conversion potential of the mass media, William H. Flanigan observes: "Actually political scientists have seldom studied the impact of the content of the mass media, and in part this neglect is a
reflection of the belief that campaigns are unimportant, that elections are decided before the campaign starts. Beyond this there is
the belief that Americans receive little political information from
the mass media or from any other source."[8]

There are a number of reasons why conversion is uncommon
even among those who are exposed to political information. Media
exposure in a campaign is highest among the most politically interested citizens, who are also the most partisan and the most likely
to have decided how they will vote.[9] Moreover, individuals tend
to perceive new political information selectively and to interpret

Public Opinion: Its Origins, Content and Impact (New York: John Wiley and
Sons, 1973), pp. 1-2.

6. Cf. Bernard Berelson, "What 'Missing the Newspaper' Means," in Wilbur
Schramm, ed., *The Process and Effects of Mass Communication* (Urbana:
University of Illinois Press, 1955), pp. 36-47.

7. Summarizing several decades of public opinion surveys, Alfred Hero
writes: "Data from the various polling organizations clearly show that the
majority of Americans have paid relatively little or no attention to most
international and national issues, and only relatively small minorities have
possessed even rudimentary information about these issues. Such failure of
knowledge and interest applies to both issue fronts, foreign and domestic."
Alfred Hero, "Public Reaction to Government Policy," chapter 2 of John
P. Robinson, Jerrold G. Rusk, and Kendra B. Head, *Measures of Political
Attitudes* (Survey Research Center, Institute for Social Research, 1968),
p. 24. For a succinct discussion of the level of political information in the
United States, see Fred I. Greenstein, *The American Party System and the
American People*, 2nd ed. (Englewood Cliffs, N.J.: Prentice-Hall, 1970), pp.
12-16.

8. William H. Flanigan, *Political Behavior of the American Electorate*, 2nd
ed. (Boston: Allyn and Bacon, 1972), p. 112.

9. For example, see Flanigan, pp. 112-115, and Bernard R. Berelson, Paul
F. Lazarsfeld, and William N. McPhee, *Voting* (Chicago: University of Chicago Press, 1966), pp. 26, 241.

it so as to conform with their existing opinions. The reinforcing impact of new information is therefore likely to outweigh the conversion effect.[10]

Credibility is an important factor in explaining opinion change or the lack of it.[11] Much campaign propaganda is probably discounted because it is perceived as coming from a self-serving politician. It is plausible that William Loeb's *Union Leader* faces the obstacle of being widely considered a biased source of political information.

Finally, any single source attempting to persuade voters (e.g., a newspaper's editorials) may face stiff competition from other sources. Personal influence is often mentioned as an effective counterweight to mass media influence. And newspapers may have to contend with conflicting information transmitted by the electronic media.

Thus far the discussion has presented reasons why we should not expect the *Union Leader* to be very effective in converting opinions. However, this argument may not be on very solid ground.

Although little research has explored the conversion impact of the mass media in political campaigns generally, state and local campaigns have received the least emphasis. Perhaps a larger number of vote intentions are changed during state and local races; and maybe the mass media play an important role in producing these conversions. Despite findings such as Mueller's (cited above), at least one study supports the hypothesis that newspaper endorsements are influential under some conditions at the state and local level.[12] But the main point is that the problem has not been investigated extensively.

10, An extensive summary of the relevant literature is provided by Joseph T. Klapper, *The Effects of Mass Communication* (Glencoe, Ill.: The Free Press, 1960).

11. For a discussion of evaluation of the source as a factor in opinion change, see Robert E. Lane and David O. Sears, *Public Opinion* (Englewood Cliffs, N.J.: Prentice-Hall, 1964), pp. 43 ff.

12. Examining the relationship between editorial endorsements and voting in the 1964 at-large election for members of the Illinois House of Representatives, James L. McDowell found strong similarities between endorsements and voting patterns in the Chicago area. Newspapers in other parts of the state were less successful, presumably because of more effective competing influ-

Moreover, voting in general elections has been researched much more thoroughly than voting in primaries. Without the operation of party identification as an important stabilizing influence on electoral choice, primary campaigns may have more media-induced conversion than general elections have.[13] On the national level Philip E. Converse and his Survey Research Center colleagues discovered considerable change in voting intentions among citizens who favored Eugene McCarthy at the time of the 1968 New Hampshire Democratic presidential primary. As new candidates entered the race and McCarthy's policy positions became more widely known, many of his early supporters later left the fold.[14] We might expect information transmitted by the mass media to be especially influential in primaries featuring little-known candidates.

As stated above, perhaps political affairs are not salient for most people; but then political opinions should be more amenable to change than more strongly held, ego-involved attitudes. Perhaps many *Union Leader* readers do not actively seek political news; but they can hardly avoid exposure to politics and the newspaper's editorial views. The fact that more politically interested people are more highly exposed to campaign information may not be important; the crucial consideration might be how many persons are exposed to a certain degree.

Furthermore, it is risky to assert that the *Union Leader* is viewed as an untrustworthy source of information by the majority of its readers. It may be that William Loeb's personal style of writing has established a close rapport with many readers and that his newspaper is perceived by them as a trusted source of political information. Readers who do not trust the *Union Leader* may forget where the distrusted information came from and over time may accept the initially rejected material.[15]

---

ences. James L. McDowell, "The Role of Newspapers in Illinois' At-Large Election," *Journalism Quarterly*, 42 (1965), 281-284.

13. Cf. Dan Nimmo, *The Political Persuaders* (Englewood Cliffs, N.J.: Prentice-Hall, 1970), pp. 3-5.

14. Philip E. Converse, Warren E. Miller, Jerrold G. Rusk, and Arthur C. Wolfe, "Continuity and Change in American Politics: Parties and Issues in the 1968 Election," *American Political Science Review*, 63 (1969), 1092 ff.

15. The results of an experiment by Hovland and Weiss lend credibility to

With respect to competition from other sources of political information, we should remember that the *Union Leader* enjoys a dominant position over television in New Hampshire as a source of information about statewide campaigns. As to the suggestion that personal influence might act as a counterweight to *Union Leader* effectiveness, it may be more legitimate to view interpersonal communication as aiding the paper's impact. Perhaps information and opinions are transmitted by the *Union Leader* to "opinion leaders," who then relay the material verbally to nonreaders of the paper.[16]

Even if opinion conversion is uncommon, it can be extremely important for the outcome of an election. The conversion during a campaign of only 3 or 4 percent of the electorate—a plausible change according to past research—can be decisive in a close election.

Moreover, more research has examined conversion than activation. However, in large part because of skepticism about the efficacy of conversion attempts, we might expect activation to be a more common effect of newspaper content. And if activation can stimulate even a small number of would-be nonvoters to vote, the impact could be felt in the election outcome. Whatever *Union Leader* influence the data may show, it would be unwise to conclude that such impact takes the form of conversion; activation of like-minded individuals may be far more important. Unfortunately, I am unable to compare the effectiveness of conversion and activation.

Thus there are reasons for being both pessimistic and optimistic about the short-term impact of the *Union Leader*. Before examining the data, however, we might observe that the absence of detectable newspaper influence during the campaign does not necessarily mean that the *Union Leader* is an insignificant force in the shaping of public opinion. Attitudes toward competing candi-

---

this statement. Carl I. Hovland and Walter Weiss, "The Influence of Source Credibility on Communication Effectiveness," *Public Opinion Quarterly*, 15 (1951), 635-650.

16. Cf. Kurt and Gladys Engel Lang, "The Mass Media and Voting," in Eugene Burdick and Arthur J. Brodbeck, eds., *American Voting Behavior* (Glencoe, Ill.: The Free Press, 1959), pp. 217-235.

dates are only one limited type of political orientation. Moreover, the most significant kinds of mass media impact may operate between campaigns and over a long time rather than during the short campaign period.[17]

Content-Voting Relationships

In order to obtain quantitative measures of the *Union Leader's* news and editorial content, I made a content analysis of the paper (including the *Sunday News*) from the beginning of 1960 through the end of 1972. For each issue during this period, I examined several leading display pages: 1, 2, 3, the back page, and the editorial page (which is the first page of the second section). Later I grouped the stories into two main categories: (1) positive or neutral stories about each candidate, usually his statements or speeches, and (2) negative stories about the candidate, usually a criticism of him by another public figure. Almost all photographs were placed in the positive-neutral category, the exceptions being the few photos that were obviously uncomplimentary. Finally, I counted editorials as either for or against each candidate (for details see Appendix C).

Since only selected key pages were examined in the analysis, figures based on this content do not necessarily reflect the total coverage of candidates in the entire newspaper. It is possible that some candidates or races are disproportionately covered in the sample pages, compared with the remainder of the paper. Thus since the sample pages are the most prominent pages, the content analysis measures display emphasis for the paper as a whole. In addition, if the content of the selected pages happens to be a random sample of total newspaper content, the analysis also represents the paper's total news coverage of candidates or campaigns.

If we exclude negative stories and photos,[18] a candidate's News

17, Cf. Lang, note 16 above, and V. O. Key, Jr., *Public Opinion and American Democracy* (New York: Alfred A. Knopf, 1964), p. 403.

18. I omitted the "negative" stories and photos because of uncertainty about which candidate is favored. The candidate being attacked might appear to be hurt, but the story does give him publicity and may arouse sympathy

Advantage Score equals the number of positive or neutral stories about him and photos of him minus the same quantity for his opponent—divided by the number of days in the campaign.[19] In order to ensure comparability in multicandidate campaigns (mainly primaries) only the opponent with the largest number of stories and photos is included in calculating the score.

Similarly, we may define an Editorial Support Score for each candidate as the sum of the number of favorable editorials for a candidate and unfavorable editorials about his opponent(s) minus the sum of unfavorable editorials about the candidate and favorable editorials for his opponent(s). (To eliminate double-counting, editorials both supporting one candidate and attacking another are counted only once, as being positive for the congratulated candidate.)

We are in a position to make systematic appraisals of the relationship between *Union Leader* editorial support for and news treatment of candidates. Many New Hampshire candidates have complained about the unfairness of the paper's news coverage. For example, 1966 Republican gubernatorial primary candidate Zandy Taft says of William Loeb:

> He's had a habit over the years of playing up the candidates he favors with front-page news stories every time they speak— there's a picture and there's a story on the front page. And those he's against, which wasn't just me, you seldom get—I don't think I got a picture in the paper for the last three months of the campaign. They just don't print them. Early in the campaign the news releases would be printed, but they're usually on page 33 in the lower left-hand corner; and as the campaign gets hot, gets

for him; or the information about him may be favorable in the eyes of some readers. For the 28 gubernatorial and senatorial campaigns analyzed, the excluded negative stories averaged 6 percent of the total number of stories and photos per campaign. The highest percentage of negative stories and photos in any campaign was 17.

19. "Number of days in the campaign" is defined as the number of issues of the paper from the first day after the candidate that was supported editorially and at least one other candidate have announced (or, if nobody was supported by the paper, from the time that any two candidates for the office have announced) until election day.

warmed up, they just fail to print them or they cut them short.[20]

On the other hand, one of Taft's opponents, Loeb-supported James J. Barry, claims:

> The *Union Leader* is fair in a campaign. While editorially they may favor one candidate against another, they always provide adequate coverage of all candidates' views and positions on issues. Of course a candidate who advocates taxes may find an editorial occasionally attacking his program; but so far as his statements are concerned and his public appearances, they're carried just as accurately and adequately as a candidate that is in a little better position with the paper because of his program.[21]

In order to assess the balance of the *Union Leader's* news coverage, we may utilize the News Advantage Score in the twelve primary and eleven general election campaigns between 1960 and 1972 in which the *Union Leader* supported one candidate editorially (as is the case for the rest of this section's data, only gubernatorial and senatorial contests are included). In eleven of twelve primaries and nine of eleven general election campaigns, the editorially supported candidate received more news coverage than his opponent—an overall total of 20 out of 23. Moreover, for each of the three deviant cases in which the editorially opposed candidate got more news coverage, the News Advantage Score was very low.[22]

Going further, we observe that the mean News Advantage Score for the editorially endorsed candidate in these primaries is .31; the general election figure is .33. In other words, in both primaries and general elections, on the average the *Union Leader*-supported candidate receives about one more news story in the sample pages than his opponent for every three issues of the paper. At the same time, we should note that there is a fairly wide variation in the News Advantage Scores for different campaigns.[23]

20. Interview with Alexander M. Taft, July 25, 1967.

21. Interview with James J. Barry, November 3, 1967.

22. These three cases were John Pillsbury in the 1962 Republican gubernatorial primary and Pillsbury in the 1962 and 1964 gubernatorial general elections.

23. The standard deviation of the News Advantage Scores is .22 for primaries and .27 for general elections.

Finally, we may inquire whether there is a strong relationship between the extent of editorial support and the extent of news coverage advantage. Do more ardently supported candidates (as measured by the Editorial Support Score) consistently receive much more favorable news treatment (as measured by the News Advantage Score) than the more weakly backed candidates? Using the technique of linear regression, we find a product-moment correlation (r)[24] of .61 between the Editorial Support Score and the News Advantage Score for the *Union Leader*-endorsed candidates in the twelve primaries. Much of this strength results, however, from one candidate with an Editorial Support Score over three times larger than the second-highest figure.[25] If this one extreme case is omitted, the value of r drops to .31.

For the *Union Leader*-backed candidates in the eleven general elections, the correlation between the Editorial Support Score and the News Advantage Score is .29. But the value of r is only .03 if one semi-extreme case is omitted.[26]

In short, candidates who are supported editorially by the *Union Leader* clearly do enjoy a significant news coverage advantage over their opponents. At the same time, the relationship between the *extent* of editorial support and the *extent* of news coverage advantage is moderate: the r for all 23 cases considered together (twelve primaries and eleven general elections) is a modest .45.

Discrepancies in news coverage may not be due entirely or mostly to biased news editing. The candidates themselves may be partly responsible for news coverage imbalance. It is probable that candidates work more closely with editorially favorable newspapers than with opposing papers. Particularly when one newspaper is an AM and the other is a PM, a candidate might decide to time his releases favorably to one paper rather than the other. A reinforcing cycle might exist, wherein more favorable news treatment by one

24. For readers who are not familiar with this type of statistical analysis, the product-moment correlation coefficient measures the strength of the relationship between two variables on a scale ranging from –1 to +1. Values approaching –1 and +1 indicate (respectively) a very strong negative and a very strong positive association between the two variables. Values near 0 indicate a very weak relationship.

25. The candidate receiving this fantastic degree of editorial support was Meldrim Thomson, Jr., in the 1970 Republican gubernatorial primary.

26. This case is Harrison R. Thyng in the 1966 senatorial general election.

newspaper leads to a candidate's "feeding" that paper his material more assiduously, thus leading to more extensive coverage in the paper. It is thus possible for a bias in news coverage to be magnified by the individual candidates.

With our two measures of *Union Leader* content, we are now in a position to inquire whether more favorable news and editorial treatment by the paper produces greater electoral success. To measure how well a candidate performs, we start with his percentage of the vote in the "Manchester city zone" as defined by the Audit Bureau of Circulations: Manchester plus the contiguous suburbs of Auburn, Bedford, Goffstown, Hooksett, and Londonderry. We then subtract his vote percentage in the rest of New Hampshire.[27] This variable contrasts the candidate's performance in the most highly concentrated *Union Leader* circulation area—where we expect the paper to have the greatest impact—with his showing in a large area with relatively sparse *Union Leader* circulation. On a per-capita basis, the paper's circulation is a bit more than four times stronger in the Manchester city zone as in the remainder of the state.[28] If the *Union Leader* has a notable impact on its readers, we would expect fairly strong relationships between each of the content measures on the one hand, and our new dependent variable measuring electoral performance, on the other.

We shall examine these relationships for the ten Republican gubernatorial and senatorial primaries from 1960 to 1972,[29] and

27. The sources for all election returns are the biennial volumes of the *State of New Hampshire Manual for the General Court* (Concord: Department of State).

28. According to 1966 Audit Bureau of Circulation figures and my estimates of 1966 population (based on a linear interpolation between the 1960 and 1970 census figures), 1966 per-capita *Union Leader* circulation was .22 in the Manchester city zone and .05 in the rest of New Hampshire. According to ABC circulation statistics and population estimates for 1972, that year's per-household *Union Leader* circulation was .71 in the Manchester city zone and .17 in the rest of the state. Another way of viewing these figures is to say that the ratio of *Union Leader* circulation strength in the Manchester city zone to the rest of the state was 4.4 in 1966 and 4.2 in 1972.

29. Only included are primaries in which at least two candidates both received at least 10 percent of the vote in either the Manchester city zone or the rest of New Hampshire. For primaries as well as general elections, the voting calculations include only candidates receiving at least 10 percent of the vote in either the Manchester city zone or the rest of New Hampshire.

Table 1
Union Leader News Advantage and Editorial Support Scores for
Union Leader-Endorsed Candidate in Republican Gubernatorial and
Senatorial Primaries, and for Republican Candidate in Guber-
natorial and Senatorial General Elections, 1960 to 1972

Primary Elections			*General Elections*		
Candidate, Year, Office	*News Advantage Score*	*Editorial Support Score*	*Candidate, Year, Office*	*News Advantage Score*	*Editorial Support Score*
Powell			Powell		
1960 Gov.	.72	.43	1960 Gov.	.71	.29
Pillsbury			S. Bridges		
1962 Gov.	-.07	.33	1960 Sen.	.51	.11
D. Bridges			Pillsbury		
1962 Sen.	.17	.23	1962 Gov.	-.02	.40
Pillsbury			Bass		
1964 Gov.	.20	.02	1962 Sen.	-.13	-.13
Barry			Cotton		
1966 Gov.	.28	.15	1962 Sen.	.16	.18
Thyng			Pillsbury		
1966 Sen.	.39	.21	1964 Gov.	-.09	.07
Thomson			Gregg		
1968 Gov.	.36	.32	1966 Gov.	-.17	.00
Thomson			Thyng		
1970 Gov.	.71	1.42	1966 Sen.	.63	1.07
Thomson			Peterson		
1972 Gov.	.17	.37	1968 Gov.	-.20	-.55
Powell			Cotton		
1972 Sen.	.23	.04	1968 Sen.	.09	.42
			Peterson		
			1970 Gov.	-.36	-.64
			Thomson		
			1972 Gov.	.62	.31
			Powell		
			1972 Sen.	.49	.35

for the thirteen gubernatorial and senatorial general elections during this period. I have dropped the two Democratic primaries from the twelve primaries considered above, since it seems preferable not to mix two distinct electorates (Republican and Democratic) in the same analysis. To the eleven general elections discussed above, I have added two other elections in which the *Union Leader* made no editorial endorsement.

Table 1 shows the News Advantage and Editorial Support Scores used as the independent variables in this analysis. For reasons I shall state shortly, I include these variables for the Republican candidates in the general elections.[30]

Figure 1 presents the relationship between the News Advantage Score and the electoral performance variable (Manchester city zone - rest of state) for the candidates receiving editorial support from the *Union Leader* in the ten Republican primaries. Figure 2 depicts the association between the Editorial Support Score and electoral performance for the same candidates.

Similarly, Figures 3 and 4 present the news advantage–voting and editorial support–voting relationships for the Republican candidates in the thirteen general elections. By including the variables for the candidates of the same party, we in effect hold constant the gross influence of party in different elections—if we assume that relative party strength for Manchester and the rest of New Hampshire has not changed greatly from 1960 to 1972. If we had used the variables for the candidates supported by the *Union Leader* ratner than the Republican (or Democratic) candidates— then, given Democratic strength in Manchester compared with the remainder of the state, the dependent variable would have fluctuated wildly according to whether a Republican or a Democrat was being supported by the *Union Leader*. It makes little difference which party's candidates were selected for Figures 3 and 4; I arbitrarily chose the Republican Party.

30. Following are the News Advantage and Editorial Support Scores for the two Democratic primaries in which the *Union Leader* endorsed a candidate and which have now been dropped from the analysis. Roger J. Crowley, Jr., 1970 Democratic gubernatorial primary: News Advantage .37, Editorial Support .27. Crowley, 1972 Democratic gubernatorial primary: News Advantage .20, Editorial Support .12.

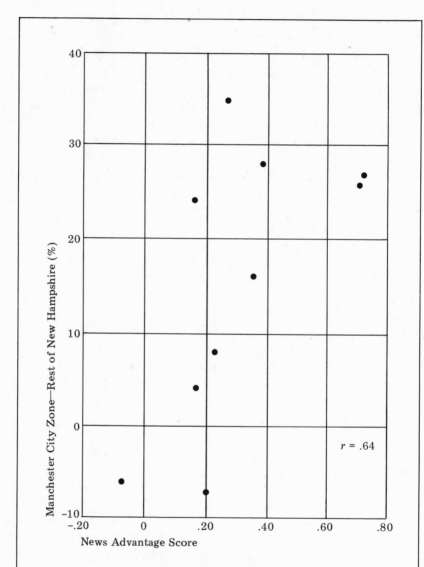

Figure 1: *Union Leader* News Advantage and
Voting for *Union Leader*-Endorsed Candidate
in Republican Gubernatorial and Senatorial
Primaries, 1960 to 1972

Readers who wish to determine which dots represent which candidates in Figures 1-4 may do so by identifying the x-axis values with the appropriate News Advantage or Editorial Support Score in Table 1. For example, the News Advantage value of -.07 for the lower-left point in Figure 1 shows that the point stands for John Pillsbury in the 1962 Republican gubernatorial primary.

In shorthand form, the product-moment correlations for Figures 1-4 run as follows:

Republican primaries, news-voting:	.64
Republican primaries, editorials-voting:	.34
General elections, news-voting:	.84
General elections, editorials-voting:	.74

It should be noted that dropping the extreme case from Figure 2 (Thomson, 1970) leaves the correlation value virtually unchanged: r equals .33 for the other nine cases. But if all ten observations are included, the association appears to be curvilinear rather than linear; r thus understates the strength of the relationship and strictly speaking is not an appropriate measure to use. The associations in Figures 1, 3, and 4 are linear, and thus r is an appropriate measure of strength in those instances.

The extreme case in Figure 2 suggests that a threshold may exist whereby *Union Leader* editorial support beyond a certain level of enthusiasm has no additional payoff in votes for the candidate. Here it appears that no amount of editorializing can push the Manchester city zone–rest of New Hampshire difference beyond the range of about 25 to 35 percent of the vote in Republican primaries. A similar though less dramatic conclusion for general elections is suggested by the right-hand semi-extreme point (Thyng 1966) in Figure 4.

On the whole the relationships in Figures 1-4 are strong. This overall strength is the most important conclusion for this section. The confidence with which we can reach this conclusion is weakened, however, by the small number of cases used to derive the correlation coefficients. Significance tests—a popular method of quantifying the degree of confidence in certain statistical conclusions—are inappropriate here because our observations (candidates or elections) are themselves a statistical population rather than a

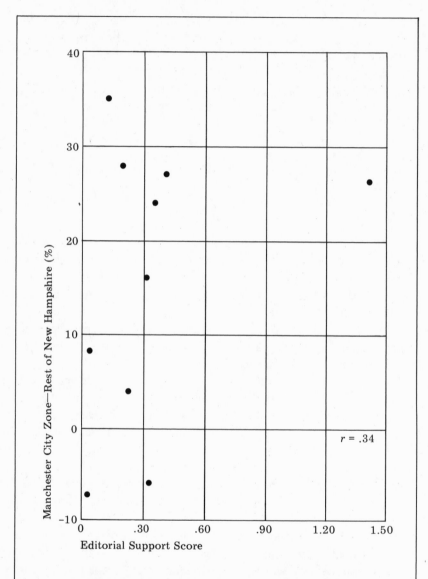

Figure 2: *Union Leader* Editorial Support and
Voting for *Union Leader*-Endorsed Candidate
in Republican Gubernatorial and Senatorial
Primaries, 1960 to 1972

random sample drawn from a larger population. Although I cannot legitimately employ significance testing to quantify my degree of confidence in the conclusions of this section, it is my interpretation that the correlation values are generally large enough to be meaningful despite the small number of cases.

For both primaries and general elections considered separately, the relationships for news coverage are greater than for editorials (.64 vs. .34 and .84 vs. .74). If these associations are valid measures of *Union Leader* influence, the interpretation of the comparisons is that news stories have more impact on the electorate than editorials. A firm conclusion of this nature is, however, unjustified: the differences between the correlations are not very meaningful given the small number of cases, especially if one assumes that the Figure 2 value (.34) understates the strength of that relationship.

In the same way, we should avoid misinterpreting the greater strength of the general election correlations, compared with the primaries (.84 and .74 vs. .64 and .34). Even if the differences were large enough to be meaningful, one must not conclude that the *Union Leader* has more impact in general elections than in Republican primaries. It should be recalled that since the candidates of only one party are used for the general election observations, the general election relationships concern marginal variations in the vote *after the factor of party has been roughly controlled.* If we did not control for the important influence of party in general elections, we would probably find that the newspaper is more effective in primaries than in general elections. That is, we would probably find that the correlations for primaries would be stronger than the uncontrolled (for party) correlations for general elections.

As always, we must be very cautious about imputing causation to the Figure 1–4 relationships. The fairly strong associations between variations in *Union Leader* content and variations in candidates' electoral performance do not necessarily mean that the first factor *causes* the second. Indeed, the associations may be at least partly spurious. For example, perhaps *Union Leader* news editors or editorial writers are attracted to the same candidates as are Manchester area residents. Maybe the editors and the voters support or oppose a given candidate to the same degree even if the news-

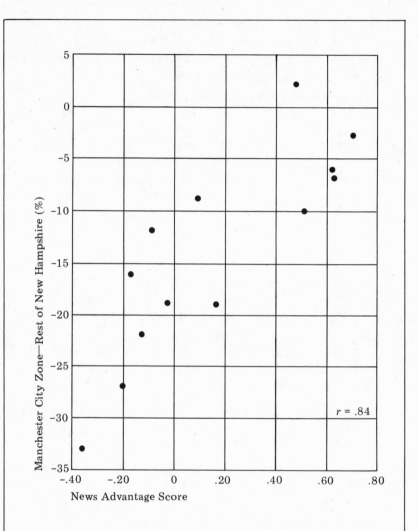

Figure 3: *Union Leader* News Advantage and
Voting for Republican Candidate in Gubernatorial
and Senatorial General Elections, 1960 to 1972

paper's content has absolutely no influence over the readership.

By way of elaboration, Manchester is widely known as a conservative community politically. Some time ago the author of a study of local politics in Manchester made an observation that still sounds appropriate: "The political life of the city is pervaded by economic conservatism. Virtually all public issues are viewed as questions of economy-in-government. The "good" public servant is one who restricts the regulatory and service functions of the municipal corporation. Above all, he must keep down taxes."[31] The political perspective is similar to that of the *Union Leader*, but it is highly likely that the existence of this community ideology is largely independent of the newspaper's activity.

Nevertheless, the observation that *Union Leader* editors and other Manchester area residents are by and large conservative does not demonstrate that this common political approach causes the variation in both *Union Leader* content and electoral performance by candidates. Indeed, basic political agreement on the part of editors and readers might be a precondition for the operation of newspaper influence. The paper might have considerable impact through the activation of like-minded readers, though not through conversion. Given the strength of the relationships in Figures 1–4, it would be surprising to me if such a close fit between *Union Leader* content and Manchester voting patterns were unaccompanied by at least *some* degree of direct causal connection between the two variables.

Besides common political beliefs of editors and readers, another possible disrupting factor is the location of candidates' campaign activities. Perhaps candidates who emphasize Manchester in their campaigning receive more news stories in the *Union Leader* and also get more votes in the Queen City—because of their campaigning, not because of the paper's news coverage; but it is implausible to an attentive reader of the *Union Leader* that the amount and prominence of its news coverage of a candidate are strongly related to the amount of time he spends campaigning in Manchester.

31. Robert H. Binstock, *A Report on Politics in Manchester, New Hampshire* (Cambridge: Joint Center for Urban Studies of the Massachusetts Institute of Technology and Harvard University, 1961), p. I-18.

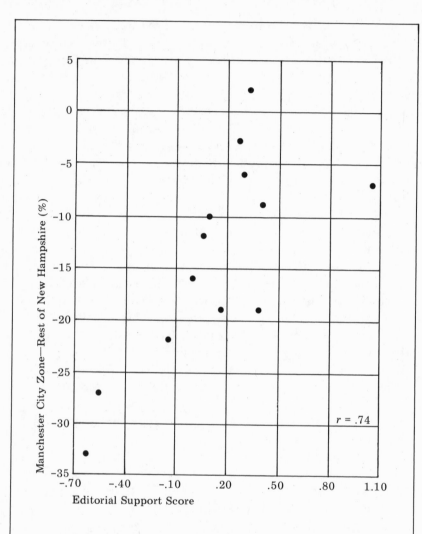

Figure 4: *Union Leader* Editorial Support and
Voting for Republican Candidate in Gubernatorial
and Senatorial General Elections, 1960 to 1972

In sum, the causal interpretation of the data of this section is tentative. The strength of the relationships is meaningful, but we cannot be certain that the high degree of association demonstrates *Union Leader* political influence on its readers.

Circulation-Voting Relationships

Adequate *Union Leader* circulation statistics for all New Hampshire towns do not exist; for many towns they are missing completely. Moreover, the figures for the towns that do have data include copies of the newspaper mailed from that town to neighboring towns. Because of this uncertainty about town circulation data and the small population of many towns, gross inaccuracies could result from using these figures. Therefore, I decided to employ New Hampshire's ten counties as the basic units of analysis. The counties are more heterogeneous than towns but have the advantage of being covered by complete circulation data.[32]

What should the correlation values between *Union Leader* circulation and the vote for candidates look like if the paper exerts influence? For primary elections we would expect moderately strong positive correlations between per-capita *Union Leader* circulation in the counties and the percentage vote for the candidate supported by the newspaper.[33] However, localism—the tendency to vote for a candidate from one's home area—may serve artifi-

32. My source for *Union Leader* circulation figures is the annual *ABC Audit Report* for the paper (Audit Bureau of Circulations, Chicago, Ill.). I had reports for the years 1962, 1964, 1966, and 1972. I estimated the 1960 circulation figures by extrapolating the 1964-to-1962 difference back two more years. My estimates for 1968 and 1970 were obtained by interpolation between the 1966 and 1972 data. I used the same method for arriving at population estimates. Starting with the 1960 and 1970 census figures, I assumed a constant (linear) rate of population increase (or decrease) during the decade and used interpolation to derive the estimates for 1962, 1964, 1966, and 1968. I extrapolated the same rate of increase/decrease to 1972 in order to obtain that year's population estimate. The changes in per-capita *Union Leader* circulation from 1960 to 1972 were very gradual for all counties.

33. The voting calculations in this section include only candidates receiving at least 10 percent of the vote in at least one county.

cially to weaken or strengthen the relationships. Hence, I calculated correlations both for all ten counties and for just the counties
that are not the home of one of the candidates.

The general election picture should be clouded by the influence
of party. Ideally we would like to have an estimate of the normally expected vote for a given party's gubernatorial or senatorial
candidate—that is, the percentage of the vote we would expect
him to win in the absence of *Union Leader* impact. We could then
compare the actual vote with the normally expected value, using
the difference as a measure of *Union Leader* influence. Unfortunately, it is very difficult to derive a good "normal vote" estimate
for most gubernatorial and senatorial elections. Previous elections
for the same office generally provide a very imperfect guide for
the normally expected vote because of large between-election variations in the operation of such influential factors as presidential
coattails, the strength of candidates' organizations, the attractive-
ness of candidates' personal characteristics, and the *Union Leader*
itself.

An admittedly rough procedure can be used to derive a general
estimate of the expected correlation in the absence of *Union
Leader* influence. We assume that the newspaper has no electoral
impact and examine the correlation (for counties) between degree
of ruralism and *Union Leader* circulation, as well as the correlation between ruralism and Republican voting strength. Multiplying
these two correlation coefficients yields a rough estimate of the
normally expected correlation between *Union Leader* circulation
and Republican voting, under the assumption that the paper has
no electoral impact.[34] Marked departures from this "normal"
value might indicate *Union Leader* influence in an election.

34. This procedure is based on the analysis of causal models suggested by
Hubert M. Blalock, Jr. In this three-variable model, ruralism can be seen as
"causing" the patterns of both *Union Leader* circulation and Republican
voting; no causal link is hypothesized between the last two variables. An
important (and rather heroic) assumption underlying the validity of this model is the absence of any fourth variable which influences more than one of
the variables in the model. See Hubert M. Blalock, Jr., *Social Statistics* (New
York: McGraw-Hill, 1960), pp. 337–343. Also Blalock, *Causal Inferences in
Nonexperimental Research* (Chapel Hill: University of North Carolina Press,
1964).

In 1960 *Union Leader* circulation had a fairly weak negative relationship with the percentage of rural inhabitants in a county.[35]
Since the rural percentage was very strongly associated with Republican voting,[36] for the early 60's we would normally expect
a fairly weak negative relationship between *Union Leader* circulation and the vote for Republican candidates in the absence of
any electoral impact by the paper. My rough estimate of this normal association between *Union Leader* circulation and Republican
voting is $r = -.30$.[37] If the newspaper backs the Republican candidate, correlation values more positive than this figure (even near
zero) might indicate *Union Leader* influence.

By 1970 the circulation-percentage of rural correlation had shifted to weakly positive.[38] At the same time ruralism was strongly
associated with Republican voting.[39] For the early 70's, therefore,
we would normally expect a weak positive relationship between
Union Leader circulation and the vote for Republicans in the absence of any electoral impact by the paper. My rough estimate of
this more recent "normal" association between *Union Leader*
circulation and Republican voting is $r = .07$.[40] Thus around 1970
moderately strong positive values might be required to indicate
Union Leader influence if the paper is supporting the Republican
candidate.

Localism is a much weaker factor in general elections than in
primaries. In the general-election correlations below I do not in-

35. $r = -.34$ (using 1960 census figures for percent rural).

36. The correlation between percent rural (1960) and percent for Richard
Nixon (1960 presidential general election) is .82. The correlation between
percent rural (1960) and percent for Perkins Bass (1962 senatorial general
election) is .93.

37. This estimate is derived by multiplying the correlation in note 35 by
each of the correlations in note 36, and then averaging the two products.

38. $r = .11$ (using 1970 census figures for percent rural).

39. The correlation between percent rural (1970) and percent for Richard
Nixon (1972 presidential general election) is .70. The correlation between
percent rural (1970) and percent for Walter Peterson *plus* percent for Meldrim Thomson (1970 gubernatorial general election) is .53. I add Peterson
and Thomson together as an indicator of Republican voting because Thomson
was a normal Republican running as a third-party candidate.

40. This estimate is derived by multiplying the correlation in note 38 by
each of the correlations in note 39, and then averaging the two products.

Table 2
Union Leader Circulation and Voting in Gubernatorial and
Senatorial Primaries and General Elections, 1960 to 1972

Primary Elections			General Elections	
	Product-Moment Correlation			
Candidate, Year Party, Office	All Counties	Non-home Counties	Candidate, Year, Office	Product-Moment Correlation
Powell,			Powell, 1960 Gov.	-.20
1960 Rep. Gov.	.13	(.18)	S. Bridges, 1960 Sen.	-.27
Pillsbury,			Pillsbury, 1962 Gov.	-.31
1962 Rep. Gov.	-.03	(-.13)	Bass, 1962 Sen.	-.27
D. Bridges,			Cotton, 1962 Sen.	-.29
1962 Rep. Sen.	.16	(.49)	Pillsbury, 1964 Gov.	.09
Pillsbury,			Gregg, 1966 Gov.	.01
1964 Rep. Gov.	.10	(-.49)	Thyng, 1966 Sen.	.23
Barry,			Peterson, 1968 Gov.	-.29
1966 Rep. Gov.	.55	(.63)	Cotton, 1968 Sen.	.09
Thyng,			Peterson, 1970 Gov.	-.74
1966 Rep. Sen.	.72	(.83)	Thomson, 1972 Gov.	.33
Thomson,			Powell, 1972 Sen.	.46
1968 Rep. Gov.	.57	(.74)		
Crowley,				
1970 Dem. Gov.	.66	(.46)		
Thomson,				
1970 Rep. Gov.	.64	(.77)		
Crowley,				
1972 Dem. Gov.	.57	(.32)		
Thomson,				
1972 Rep. Gov.	.75	(.85)		
Powell,				
1972 Rep. Sen.	.42	(.81)		

clude separate figures for the counties that are not the home of
one of the candidates. "Non-home" county correlations that do
not include Hillsborough County (Manchester) depart wildly from
the all-county correlations because the former omit a county that
is both strongly Democratic and has a strong *Union Leader* circu-

lation. Hence the "non-home" relationships for general elections
are not very meaningful.

Table 2 presents the product-moment correlations (for the ten
counties) between per-capita *Union Leader* circulation and the
percentage vote for the *Union Leader*-endorsed candidate (in the
case of primaries) and for the Republican candidate (in general
elections). Included are all thirteen gubernatorial and senatorial
general elections from 1960 to 1972, as well as the twelve primaries (ten Republican and two Democratic) in which the newspaper endorsed a candidate.

·The correlations for the primaries are generally strong, especially in recent years. There is notable strength in the relationships
for Harrison Thyng and Meldrim Thomson, two relative unknowns
who were given massive support by the *Union Leader*. Distinguish-
ing between "home" and "non-home" counties, Figures 5 and 6
picture the strongest correlations from Table 2: Thyng in the 1966
Republican senatorial primary and Thomson in the 1972 Republican gubernatorial primary. The influence of localism is evident in
these graphs, especially in the Thyng election.

Given the small number of Democratic primaries during the
1960–1972 period, we are unable meaningfully to compare *Union
Leader* impact in Democratic and Republican primaries.

The weaker and more negative correlations in general elections,
as compared with primaries, indicate the importance of party identification as a competing factor which limits *Union Leader* influence in general elections. The general-election correlations bear
out the expectation of a modest "normal" shift in the positive
direction from 1960 to 1972. At the same time, significant *Union
Leader* impact is suggested by some marked departures from the
normally expected value (i.e. the approximate correlation value
expected if the paper exerts no influence). Specifically, the correlations for Harrison Thyng (1966), Meldrim Thomson (1972),
and Wesley Powell (1972) are stronger than the normally expected
value; the *Union Leader* supported all three candidates. And the
negative correlations for Loeb-opposed Walter Peterson (1968 and
1970) suggest that the paper had an effect in these elections also.
Indeed, the drastic shift in the correlations for the Republican
gubernatorial candidates in the consecutive 1970 and 1972 elections—from -.74 for Loeb-opposed Walter Peterson in 1970 to .33

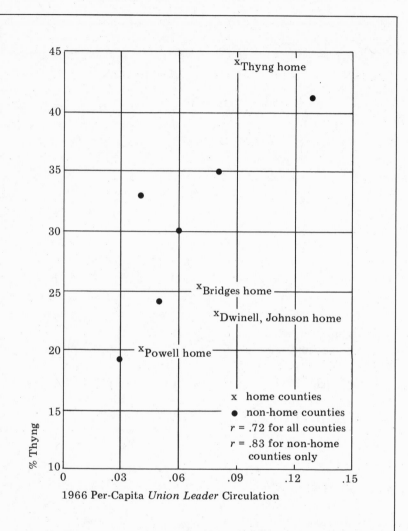

Figure 5: *Union Leader* Circulation and the Thyng Vote, 1966 Republican Senatorial Primary, for Counties

for Loeb-backed Meldrim Thomson in 1972—is highly suggestive
of *Union Leader* impact. However, the 1970 and 1972 gubernatorial correlations may have been distorted in some way by the
unusual presence of a third-party or independent candidate in
both elections (Thomson in 1970 and Malcolm McLane in 1972).

By comparing the performances of general election candidates
from the same party, we are in effect holding party constant and
examining residual variations which might indicate *Union Leader*
influence. According to our news advantage and editorial support
data, on two occasions from 1960 to 1972 the *Union Leader*
adopted sharply contrasting stances toward Republican senatorial
and gubernatorial running mates in the same general election: in
1966 the paper strongly backed Harrison Thyng while remaining
neutral with regard to Hugh Gregg, and in 1968 Loeb ardently supported Norris Cotton while strongly opposing Walter Peterson.
The Table 2 correlations support the hypothesis that *Union Leader*
impact operated for both comparisons.

Another way of approaching the Thyng-Gregg and Cotton-Peterson vote differences is to correlate these quantities (Thyng minus
Gregg and Cotton minus Peterson) with *Union Leader* circulation.
These correlations are strongly positive (.58 for the 1966 case and
.79 for 1968), as shown by Figures 7 and 8; indeed, the value of
r may underestimate the strength of the Thyng-Gregg case because
of the curvilinearity of the relationship. Once again the hypothesis
of positive *Union Leader* influence is supported.

A similar operation examines the change in Democrat John
King's vote from 1966 to 1968. Having been praised by the *Union
Leader* for his performance as governor, King was neither endorsed
nor opposed by Loeb in his 1966 reelection campaign against Hugh
Gregg. However, two years later the *Union Leader* strongly supported Norris Cotton, King's opponent in the senatorial contest.
If the newspaper exerted an impact in these two elections, we
would expect a negative correlation between *Union Leader* circulation and the 1968 King vote minus the 1966 King vote. The actual relationship is negative but not very strong: $r = -.37$ for 1966
Union Leader circulation and $-.29$ for 1968 circulation.

Finally, one case is promising for the use of partial correlation
as a technique for detecting *Union Leader* influence with party

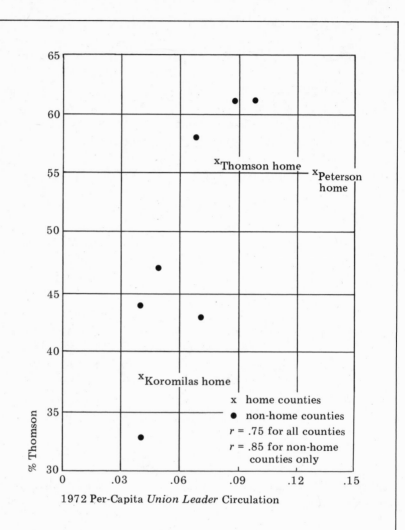

Figure 6: *Union Leader* Circulation and the Thomson Vote, 1972 Republican Gubernatorial Primary, for Counties

held constant in general elections. Let us start with the fairly weak
Table 2 correlation of .23 for Harrison Thyng in 1966. Is the relationship between *Union Leader* circulation and the Thyng vote
stronger when party is taken into account? As a measure of normal Republican Party strength for this office we take the vote of
the Republican candidate in the previous off-year senatorial election, Perkins Bass in 1962. The Bass vote is also attractive as a
measure of normally expected Republican voting in Thyng's election because Bass and Thyng faced the same opponent, Thomas
McIntyre. Indeed, a very strong (but far from perfect) correlation
of .84 exists between the Bass vote and the Thyng vote. Combining
this value and the correlations of Bass and Thyng with 1966 *Union
Leader* circulation, we see whether a strong association exists between circulation and the Thyng general election vote when party
is controlled through partial correlation. The original value of .23
jumps to .68 when party is controlled in this way—another indication of *Union Leader* impact.

The values of the correlations reported in the preceding three
paragraphs are roughly as strong as the Table 2 values for primaries. In other words, the general-election impact of the *Union
Leader* with party controlled is about as strong as the newspaper's
primary-election influence. But in practical terms the Loeb press
appears to be more important in primaries, which unlike general
elections do not include the powerful competing influence of party identification.

A different approach to investigating *Union Leader* impact in
primaries is to ask whether the Table 2 correlations are stronger
for the candidates receiving more news and editorial support. We
may compare the rankings of the candidates' News Advantage
Scores and Editorial Support Scores (presented in Table 1) with
the rankings of the candidates' Table 2 correlations. There is indeed a positive correspondence between these rankings, but the
relationships are weak. For the ten Republican primaries the Spear-
man rank-order correlation between the extent of news coverage
advantage and the Table 2 correlations is .31 (.19 for non-home
counties). The analogous rank-order correlation for editorial support is .24 (.15 for non-home counties).

So far our investigation of voting patterns has said nothing about

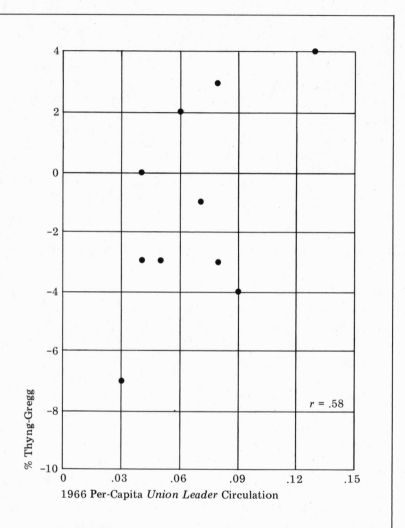

Figure 7: *Union Leader* Circulation and the Thyng-Gregg Vote Difference, 1966 General Election, for Counties

Union Leader influence on election outcomes. It is interesting to note that the paper backed eight winners and four losers in the primaries listed in Table 2; and in the general elections the Loeb press has supported five winners and six losers among the eleven endorsed candidates. Of course it would be naive to measure the impact of a newspaper by the number of winners it has supported. A paper might make a difference, however, in a close election. Using the Table 2 correlations as a rough indicator of *Union Leader* impact and examining election margins, it is plausible that Loeb influenced the outcomes of four gubernatorial or senatorial primaries from 1960 to 1972. The victorious candidates who might not have won without *Union Leader* support were Powell (1960), Thyng (1966), Crowley (1970), and Thomson (1972). During this period there was only one general election in which I think the *Union Leader* might have influenced the outcome: Thomson's 1972 victory (although Loeb may have indirectly influenced one or two other general elections by helping to nominate a weak candidate who then lost). But as in any close election, one could argue that any one of many factors besides the newspaper made the difference in the outcome.

Although on the whole this section's circulation-voting data seem to indicate considerable *Union Leader* impact on the electorate, I must again introduce a note of caution about drawing causal inferences.

Perhaps individuals with political beliefs similar to those of the *Union Leader* buy the paper, while those who disagree with the paper's political approach do not subscribe. Perhaps many conservative citizens buy the paper and also vote for conservative candidates supported by the *Union Leader*, although these people may not be influenced by the Loeb press in their voting. In other words, political conservatism might influence both the decision to subscribe to the *Union Leader* and voting decisions, but the latter two kinds of actions may not be connected by a direct causal link. If this pattern is repeated frequently enough in some areas of New Hampshire, the causal connection between *Union Leader* circulation and voting could be more apparent than real.

The case for *Union Leader* impact would be strengthened if one could show that only a very small number of people buy the news-

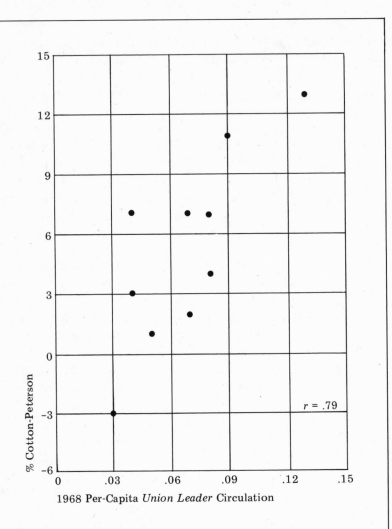

Figure 8: *Union Leader* Circulation and the Cotton-Peterson Vote Difference, 1968 General Election, for Counties

paper because they agree with its political views. We might start
by assuming that whenever possible people buy a local daily newspaper because of the local news and the advertising, not for the
political content. But in New Hampshire many areas are served
only by the *Union Leader*, the single daily newspaper with statewide distribution. We might expect *Union Leader* circulation to
be highest in its home city, lowest in the cities with evening dailies, and about the same elsewhere. Indeed, the newspaper virtually
saturates Manchester and has its lowest circulation in the evening
daily cities, but its circulation is far from uniform in other areas.
The degree of variation in *Union Leader* circulation among such
areas in different counties does not contradict the hypothesis that
most people decide to buy the *Union Leader* on the basis of their
political views.

A different conclusion, however, is reached through one bit of
survey data. The students in a Dartmouth College voting behavior
seminar taught by Professors Roger H. Davidson and David M.
Kovenock conducted a survey of 360 randomly selected respondents throughout New Hampshire approximately two weeks before
the 1968 presidential primary. Newspaper readers were asked
which candidate their paper supported. At the time of the survey
George Romney had not yet withdrawn from the race. Although
the *Union Leader* had attacked Romney vigorously throughout
the second half of 1967, it did not launch an all-out editorial war
in the months preceding the primary election. Nevertheless, there
was ample indication that it supported Richard M. Nixon. During
the three-month period prior to Romney's withdrawal, the paper
printed five predominantly pro-Nixon editorials and eight editorials attacking Romney.[41]

In the survey 39 percent of 127 *Union Leader* readers polled
were able to name Nixon as the candidate backed by the newspaper; 57 percent said they did not know whom the *Union Leader*
was supporting; and 4 percent named an incorrect candidate.[42]

41. Although Loeb was to attack Eugene McCarthy strongly in the closing
days of the primary campaign, at the time of the survey the *Union Leader*
had paid very little editorial attention to the Democratic contest between
McCarthy and backers of Lyndon B. Johnson.
42. This survey is unpublished. Its results were kindly made available to me

It seems to me that any reader who did not know that the *Union Leader* was supporting Nixon was not sufficiently aware politically to have subscribed to the paper for political reasons. Proceeding on this assumption, we are left with a maximum of about 40 percent of *Union Leader* subscribers who might have selected the newspaper because they agreed with its political views. This figure drops to 20 percent if we assume that subscribers residing in the Manchester area, about half the total, select the newspaper not for political reasons but because it is the local paper. This 20 percent figure shrinks even more if we assume that many New Hampshirites are unable to choose between newspapers but must read the *Union Leader* if they want a daily paper. Based on this reasoning, it is highly implausible to me that more than 5 percent of *Union Leader* subscribers in the state read the paper primarily because they agree with its political views;[43] and this number is far too small to invalidate the relationships between *Union Leader* circulation and voting patterns.

Nevertheless, political self-selection could enter the correlations through nonreaders who stay away from the *Union Leader* because of their disagreement with its political approach. The number of such persons probably would not be high enough to be significant, but the possibility should be recognized.

Other factors could account for the strong correspondence between *Union Leader* circulation and voting for its favorite candidates. For example, perhaps the paper's circulation is most heavily concentrated in more conservative parts of the state, for reasons having nothing to do with political self-selection. Unfortunately, the causal interpretation of the data presented in this section (as well as the preceding section) remains tentative.

---

by Professors Davidson and Kovenock. Unfortunately, I was unable to obtain access to additional public opinion polling data which might have shed light on *Union Leader* influence.

43. I think that this conclusion is consistent with the possibility that a larger percentage of readers are sometimes influenced by the *Union Leader*, especially when the newspaper crusades more vigorously than in this presidential primary election.

Trends over Time

Is there evidence that *Union Leader* influence has increased or de-
creased through time? Is there evidence of cumulative impact span-
ning a series of elections?

Bearing in mind the dangers of drawing causal inferences from
the data in Table 2, we observe a definite trend in the strengthen-
ing of that table's correlations from 1960 to 1972. The *Union
Leader* circulation-voting relationships for primaries are markedly
stronger from 1966 on than they are from 1960 to 1964. And the
associations for general elections are in line with the "normally"
expected values in the early 60's, but the numbers depart sharply
from the "normal" values in more recent years. At least we may
say that the Table 2 correlations do not contradict the hypothesis
that *Union Leader* impact has increased from 1960 to 1972.

A promising examination of *Union Leader* influence over time
concerns the political career of Wesley Powell, who ran for governor or United States senator every two years between 1950 and
1972, with the exception of 1952 and 1970. A flamboyant and
controversial personality, Powell was ardently supported by the
Union Leader from his first race in 1950 through 1960. In the
latter year Powell gained reelection to his second two-year term
as governor. William Loeb dramatically turned against him, however, when he refused to appoint Loeb's choice, Mrs. Doloris
Bridges, to the Senate after the late 1961 death of her husband,
Styles Bridges.

Loeb's opposition was extremely bitter in the 1962 gubernatorial primary, which Powell lost. From 1964 through 1968 the publisher largely ignored Powell, though a few sharply critical editorials
punctuated the silence. After staying on the sidelines in 1970 and
supporting Loeb-endorsed gubernatorial candidate Meldrim Thomson, Jr., Powell enjoyed enthusiastic *Union Leader* backing in his
successful 1972 senatorial primary and his unsuccessful general
election campaign against Thomas McIntyre.

Our data allow us to examine *Union Leader* circulation and
Powell's electoral performance in primaries from 1960 to 1972.

Table 3
Union Leader Circulation and Voting for Wesley Powell in
Gubernatorial and Senatorial Primaries, 1960 to 1972

Product-Moment Correlation

Year	All Counties	Non-home Counties
1960	.13	.18
1962	.03	.13
1964	-.10	.49
1966	-.31	-.13
1968	-.23	.25
1972	.42	.81

If we adopt the correlation between circulation and the Powell vote as the measure of *Union Leader* influence, and hypothesize that the paper has a significant impact, we expect a sharp negative movement of the correlation from 1960 to 1962. After continued and perhaps increasingly strong negative correlations throughout the rest of the decade, we anticipate a dramatic, positive reversal of the value for 1972. Table 3 presents the relevant correlations for New Hampshire's ten counties.

Our expectations are partially fulfilled. There is no significant change from 1960 to 1962, though the correlations for all counties move in the negative direction later in the decade. However, the 1972 correlations rise sharply and positively, as we predicted.

Figure 9 employs our other indicator of *Union Leader* impact—variations of the vote in the Manchester city zone compared with the rest of the state—by tracing Powell's electoral performance from 1950 to 1972. Possible *Union Leader* influence is suggested by Powell's dramatic improvement in Manchester from 1950 to 1954; perhaps Loeb's support helped him become known more quickly and more favorably in the Queen City than he would have in the absence of the newspaper's backing.

Despite a small setback in 1958, Powell's relative performance in Manchester continued to rise and reached a dramatic peak in 1960. In that year's gubernatorial primary the *Union Leader* waged

a furious news and editorial battle for Powell and against his opponent, Hugh Gregg. (It is interesting to note that Gregg was also
Powell's opponent in 1958, when Powell ran less well in Manchester.)

The steep decline in Powell's relative Manchester vote after Loeb
turned against Powell in 1961 suggests possible *Union Leader* influence. Powell's relative vote hit bottom for the decade in the
1966 senatorial primary, when Loeb enthusiastically boosted General Thyng. Powell reversed his slide in the 1968 gubernatorial
primary, however, even though the *Union Leader* strongly supported Meldrim Thomson. Moreover, contrary to our hypothesis
of *Union Leader* impact, the vote for Powell was only slightly
better in 1972, when he once again had Loeb's blessing. On the
other hand, one could argue that the 1972 value is artificially low
because of the localism effect produced by one of Powell's senatorial primary opponents, Manchester native David Brock.

In sum our evidence gives support to the hypothesis of cumulative *Union Leader* impact in the case of Wesley Powell, although
the results are not so clear-cut as we might have expected.

The data also suggest that the *Union Leader* may have exerted a
cumulative impact on the electorate in the case of Loeb favorite
Meldrim Thomson. A relative newcomer to statewide politics,
Thomson lost close Republican gubernatorial primaries in 1968
and 1970 before winning the 1972 primary and general election.
Though the differences are not large, the Table 2 circulation-
voting correlations for counties lend at least a weak measure of
support to the proposition that the *Union Leader* was more influential on Thomson's behalf as time progressed. The relevant correlations for the 1968, 1970 and 1972 primaries are (respectively)
.57, .64, and .75 (for all counties) and .74, .77, and .85 (for "non-
home" counties only). Firmer support for the cumulative-influence
hypothesis comes from examining the changes in Thomson's vote
from 1968 to 1972. The correlations between 1970 *Union Leader*
circulation and the 1972 minus 1968 difference are .35 (for all
counties) and a fairly strong .65 for "non-home" counties only.

The contrast of the Thomson vote in the Manchester city zone
compared with the rest of New Hampshire suggests greater *Union
Leader* impact after 1968, though there is little difference between

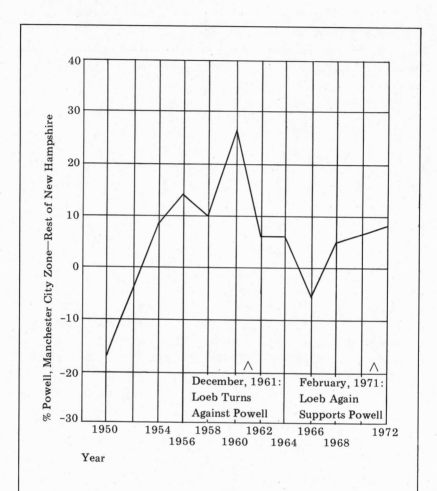

Figure 9: The Powell Vote in Republican
Gubernatorial and Senatorial Primaries, 1950
to 1972

1970 and 1972. In the 1968 primary Thomson ran 16 percent more strongly in Manchester than in the rest of the state; the comparable figures for 1970 and 1972 are (respectively) 26 percent and 24 percent. On the whole, the Thomson data suggest that the *Leader* can exert a cumulative influence through time.

Our final inspection of longitudinal data starts with the proposition that if vigorous *Union Leader* advocacy has had an electoral impact, we should be able to detect certain changes in voting patterns by comparing the elections before William Loeb bought the newspaper in late 1946 with the elections since then. The pre-Loeb *Leader* was not a crusading newspaper. One approach is to examine the voting difference between Manchester and a politically similar New Hampshire city. The goal is to study two cities whose basic political differences have not changed. We thus hope to hold political predispositions constant and treat the change in *Union Leader* ownership as the independent variable. We predict that voting differences between the two cities have increased since Loeb's arrival and have increased in the direction of Loeb-backed candidates having done better in Manchester.

The city selected for comparison with Manchester is Nashua, the state's second largest city (1970 population 56,000 compared with Manchester's 88,000). The two cities are fairly close to each other in regard to socioeconomic statistics (some illustrative figures are presented below). Both Manchester and Nashua are predominantly industrial cities and have been Democratic strongholds for many years.

For our dependent variable we start with the average absolute difference between Manchester and Nashua in the percentage vote for each candidate in an election, averaged for all the candidates. One number measuring the voting discrepancy between the two cities is thus derived for each electoral contest.[44] We then com-

44. For example, if Candidate A beats Candidate B in Manchester by a percentage total of 60-40 and Candidate A wins in Nashua by 57-43, the difference score is $3 = (3 + 3)/2$. If three candidates are running in a primary and their respective vote percentages are 48-38-14 in Manchester and 45-35-20 in Nashua, the difference score is $4 = (3 + 3 + 6)/3$. This definition of the difference measure allows us to compare primaries having different numbers of candidates running. The analysis excludes candidates failing to win at least 10 percent of the vote in at least one of the two cities.

Table 4

Mean Voting Differences between Manchester and Nashua before and after William Loeb's Purchase of the *Union Leader*

All Elections

	Primaries	General Elections
1928–46	12.8 (*N* = 19)	4.1 (*N* = 16)
1948–66	19.3 (*N* = 18)	6.8 (*N* = 19)

"Non-Hometown" Elections Only

	Primaries	General Elections
1928–46	8.2 (*N* = 14)	3.9 (*N* = 8)
1948–66	13.3 (*N* = 8)	6.7 (*N* = 14)

pute the average difference score for the races in the ten election years since Loeb obtained control of the *Union Leader* and compare this figure with the average absolute difference for the ten elections prior to Loeb's appearance (I chose the total of ten arbitrarily). The two time periods to be compared are thus 1928 to 1946 and 1948 to 1966.[45] We predict that the average difference between Manchester and Nashua is greater for the more recent period than for the earlier years.

Table 4 presents the comparison between the two time periods for gubernatorial and senatorial primaries and general elections. Figures are given for all elections and also for "non-hometown" elections only; the latter are defined as elections in which neither candidate comes from Manchester or Nashua, or else both candidates come from the same city. This control for the influence of localism makes little difference for general elections but does affect the figures for primaries.

All comparisons indicate a change in the direction of greater contrast between the two cities; the hypothesis of Loeb impact

45. I included the 1946 general election in the earlier time period, since Loeb bought the *Union Leader* only days before that election.

is supported. However, the numbers of cases are not sufficiently large to permit us unbounded confidence in these results.[46]

The interpretation that Table 4 demonstrates *Union Leader* impact is on shaky ground if the differences between Manchester and Nashua since 1948 have not generally gone in the direction of the Loeb-backed candidates' having done better in Manchester. However, the data resolve this question in favor of *Union Leader* impact. From 1950 (the first year of *Leader* files I was able to obtain) until 1966, the newspaper took an editorial position in twelve primary contests. Eight of the endorsed candidates ran better in Manchester, and four were more successful in Nashua. The *Union Leader* record becomes slightly better if "non-home-town" primaries only are included: in these elections five *Leader*-endorsed candidates ran more strongly in Manchester, two in Nashua.[47] The corresponding figures for *Leader*-endorsed general election candidates are eleven and one.[48] The overall record for "non-hometown" primaries and general elections combined is impressive: sixteen *Leader*-backed candidates did better in Manchester, three in Nashua. The case for *Union Leader* impact is strengthened by the fact that for the "non-hometown" primaries the five largest differences between Manchester and Nashua include Loeb-supported candidates who ran better in Manchester.[49]

46. For the same reasons as stated above during the discussion of Figures 1-4, significance testing is inappropriate for the present data.

47. These two exceptions are the 1950 Republican senatorial primary and the 1954 Democratic gubernatorial primary. The two Loeb-backed candidates who were more successful in Nashua than in Manchester were, respectively, Wesley Powell and Charles R. Eastman.

48. The deviant case is the 1962 gubernatorial general election, in which Loeb-supported John Pillsbury did slightly better in Nashua. The 1952 gubernatorial general election was not audited and is not included in the present figures.

49. These candidates are Wesley Powell (1954 and 1956), John Shaw (1960), Doloris Bridges (1962), and Harrison R. Thyng (1966).

The largest Manchester-versus-Nashua difference in the entire 1928-66 period demonstrates the joint operation of localism and ardent *Union Leader* support. In 1960 Wesley Powell enjoyed the benefits of a Loeb crusade on his behalf while running against Nashuan Hugh Gregg in the Republican gubernatorial primary. Powell carried Manchester by 75-25, while Gregg took

Table 5

Mean Voting Differences between Manchester and Nashua:
1948–1958 vs. 1960–1972

All Elections

	Primaries	*General Elections*
1948–58	16.7 (*N* = 10)	7.1 (*N* = 11)
1960–72	23.2 (*N* = 15)	8.5 (*N* = 13)

"Non-Hometown" Elections Only

	Primaries	*General Elections*
1948–58	11.6 (*N* = 5)	6.7 (*N* = 7)
1960–72	23.6 (*N* = 7)	7.4 (*N* = 8)

The same is true for the two largest general election differences.[50]

Extending the analysis through 1972, we may ask whether *Leader* influence has increased during the period since Loeb bought the paper. Table 5 attempts to answer this question by comparing the Manchester-Nashua differences for 1948 to 1958 and 1960 to 1972. A steady increase in *Leader* impact should make the average differences larger in the latter time period.

The figures for primaries indicate a substantial widening of the difference between Manchester and Nashua—again, in the direction of Loeb-endorsed candidates performing better in Manchester. For general elections there is a slight tendency toward increased differences between the two cities. However, I arbitrarily included the 1960 elections in the later time period rather than the earlier one. If we take as the two periods 1948–60 and 1962–72, the mean differences between the two for general elections virtually disappear and indeed run slightly in the opposite direction—toward a decreasing gap between Manchester and Nashua rather than an increasing difference.

Nashua by 82–18. The strengths of the candidates' organizations in the two cities (a factor to be discussed below) also undoubtedly contributed to this electoral pattern.

50. Wesley Powell in 1958 and 1960.

Hence the data are consistent with the hypothesis that for primaries *Union Leader* impact has increased during the period since Loeb purchased the paper. There has been almost no change, however, for general elections. Moreover, for both primaries and general elections the numbers of cases are too small to warrant very firm conclusions.

The assumption underlying this discussion has been that greater differences between election outcomes in Manchester and Nashua since Loeb's purchase of the *Union Leader* demonstrate the newspaper's impact, although it is possible that the overall pattern of increasing vote polarization between the two cities has been caused by factors having nothing to do with *Leader* influence. For example, in the last fifteen to twenty years Nashua has attracted more modern industry than Manchester and has been more dynamic economically. From 1950 to 1970 Nashua's population grew by 61 percent, while Manchester's increased by only 6 percent. During the 60's the population of Nashua expanded by 43 percent, while Manchester's shrank slightly. Perhaps economic and demographic changes have produced some political differences that had not existed between the cities in earlier years.

Table 6 presents several socioeconomic comparisons between Manchester and Nashua for 1960 and 1970. The average income gap between the two cities has been growing for some time. Adding 1950 census data to the Table 6 figures, we observe that in 1950 the median family income was about $50 higher in Manchester than in Nashua; but in 1960 it was about $300 higher in Nashua, and in 1970 the Nashua advantage was almost $1400. The relative position of the two cities with respect to median school years completed changed very little between 1960 and 1970; but in 1940 only 0.1 year separated the two cities on this variable, compared with 0.7 year in 1970.[51]

Though it would be risky to assume that political differences automatically ensue from the increasing socioeconomic differentiation between Manchester and Nashua, the contrast between the

51. These socioeconomic data are derived from the *Characteristics of the Population* (in 1970 the *General Social and Economic Characteristics*), part of the decennial census compiled by the U.S. Bureau of the Census (Washington: Government Printing Office) for the years from 1940 through 1970.

Table 6

Selected Socioeconomic Comparisons between Manchester and
Nashua for 1960 and 1970

1960	Manchester	Nashua
Foreign stock population	43.9%	40.5%
Median family income	$5,796	$6,108
Family income less than $3,000	– 13.8%	11.8%
Family income greater than $10,000	11.6%	13.9%
Median school years completed	9.3	9.9

1970		
Foreign stock population	36.2%	30.7%
Median family income	$9,489	$10,866
Family income less than $3,000	7.9%	5.2%
Family income greater than $10,000	45.8%	57.5%
Median school years completed	11.5	12.2

two cities in presidential general elections has been growing during
the past two decades. In the nine elections from 1928 to 1956,
the average presidential vote difference between Manchester and
Nashua was just under 2.5 percent. However, for the four presidential elections from 1960 to 1972, the average difference shot
up to almost 9 percent. Between 1928 and 1956 the largest spread
between the two cities in any presidential election (rounded off to
the nearest percentage point) was 4 percent. But the percentage
differences for the next four elections were, respectively, five, sev-
en, nine, and fourteen. Moreover, there is a consistent pattern in
this growing differentiation. In each of the recent elections Nashua
has supported the Democratic (more liberal) candidate more heavily than Manchester.

Perhaps the *Union Leader* is largely responsible for this increasing divergence between the two cities in presidential elections. To
me, however, it seems much more likely that the *Union Leader*
and other local communications media have very little influence
on voting for president. If this assumption is correct, then perhaps

the growing political differentiation between Manchester and
Nashua at the state political level has been caused by factors other
than the *Leader*. Thus while I think it is *possible* that the data of
Tables 4 and 5 demonstrate *Leader* impact, other factors may have
been more important.

Short-run campaign influences might form part of the explanation for the growing political separation between Manchester
and Nashua. Perhaps the strong Manchester performances of conservative candidates who happen to be supported by the *Union
Leader* are due to excellent campaign organizations in Manchester,
for reasons entirely divorced from the newspaper. Wesley Powell
is reputed to have had a strong organization in Manchester for a
number of elections. A 1966 campaign aide of Harrison Thyng
attributed the General's excellent showing in Manchester to his
hard-working local campaigners; this man was highly skeptical of
the notion that the *Leader* can account for voting differences between Manchester and Nashua.[52]

One of Thyng's Republican primary opponents felt, however,
that he had difficulty organizing in Manchester in large part because of a hostile atmosphere created by the *Union Leader*.[53] The
newspaper may therefore be a facilitating condition for the operation of other factors directly influencing the electorate. Much of
the Manchester-Nashua voting spread can be attributed to organi-
zational strength, but this variable might operate more effectively
because of conditions created in part by the *Leader*.

It is likely that the various indicators of *Union Leader* influence
employed in this section measure more than the paper's impact.
At the same time, perhaps the Loeb press has accelerated trends
that may have occurred in the absence of the *Union Leader*. For
example, there may have been a long-term trend toward increasing
political differentiation between Manchester and Nashua if the
Leader had not existed; but maybe the newspaper has accentuated
this trend and produced a larger political gap between the two
cities than otherwise would have occurred. At least this section's
data do not contradict the proposition that the *Union Leader* has

52. Interview, not for attribution, August 10, 1967.
53. Interview with William R. Johnson, August 9, 1967.

a significant cumulative impact over time. In any case, it is risky to view the paper as an isolated influence divorced from a broader social, economic, and political context.

The Union Leader and Presidential Elections

In its editorials the *Union Leader* paid very little attention to the 1960 Democratic and Republican primaries, as neither John F. Kennedy nor Richard M. Nixon faced serious opposition. Paul C. Fisher, Kennedy's main opponent, received some favorable editorial mentions and sympathetic news treatment, but the *Leader* did not endorse Fisher. At the same time, it was clear that the paper was unenthusiastic about Kennedy.

From mid-1960 on, the paper warmed up for the general election campaign with frequent anti-Kennedy editorials and news items. Although Nixon was not Loeb's idea of a perfect candidate, there was no doubt about where the publisher stood in the presidential race: "While, as we have said in the past, this newspaper disagrees on a number of points with Vice President Nixon, nevertheless—as Sen. Barry Goldwater repeatedly has said—'No one in his right mind' could vote for Kennedy."[54]

Loeb's main anti-Kennedy theme was that JFK did not understand the communist menace and was dangerously soft on communism. The publisher argued repeatedly that Kennedy's election would endanger American national security. A secondary theme in Loeb's campaign editorials was that JFK was a spoiled rich boy who had never learned restraint in the spending of money.[55]

Winding up his campaign in Manchester, Kennedy vigorously attacked Loeb and his "pet governor" (Wesley Powell) in a speech two days before the election. The Democratic candidate asserted that he could not think of an American newspaper "more irresponsible" than the *Union Leader* and that he could not think of a publisher "who has less regard for the truth" than Loeb. The *Leader* published Kennedy's attack together with a response by

54. "Only One Possible Choice," *Union Leader* (July 30, 1960), p. 1.
55. A good example of this approach is "Maybe Joe Will Adopt Us" *Union Leader* (October 14, 1960), p. 1.

Loeb in which he called JFK a "spoiled brat."[56] In my 1967 interview Loeb gleefully recounted this exchange with the man he attacked frequently after Kennedy assumed the presidency.[57]

A neighbor of New Hampshire, Kennedy ran well in the general election. But he still lost the state to Nixon by 20,000 votes out of a total of almost 300,000 votes cast.[58]

The year 1964 witnessed the *Leader's* most ardent crusade for a presidential candidate in the 1960–72 period. The recipient of this support was Senator Barry M. Goldwater. From mid-1963 on, the *Leader* delivered a steady barrage of news and editorial material favoring Goldwater and attacking his chief opponent for the Republican nomination, Governor Nelson A. Rockefeller. Loeb heartily endorsed Goldwater's brand of conservatism and his policy proposals, both foreign and domestic: here at last was a serious presidential contender who appreciated the communist threat and would halt America's slide toward socialism.

The publisher charged Rockefeller with some of the same faults Loeb had found in Kennedy. Indeed, in a mid-1963 editorial Loeb made the comparison explicit: like JFK, Rockefeller was a spoiled, rich glamor-boy who had socialistic tendencies and failed to appreciate the value of money. In the same editorial Loeb jumped on Rockefeller's recent divorce and remarriage as a sign that the candidate was morally flawed: "We have never had a wife-swapper in the White House and this newspaper may be wrong. However, we believe that, even though we are inhabiting an age of loose morals, the people will not accept a wife-swapper as President."[59]

Throughout the following fall and winter, Loeb continued to use an anti-upper-class appeal against Rockefeller. For example: "Actually this snob from New York just wants to kid us peasants along until he gets New Hampshire's votes and then the royal train will move on and we will get the back of his hand."[60] The

56. "Raps Loeb in Bitter Attack," *Union Leader* (November 8, 1960), p. 1.

57. Interview with William Loeb, October 23, 1967.

58. The election returns in this section are taken from the biennial volumes of the *State of New Hampshire Manual for the General Court* (Concord: Department of State).

59. " 'Which Twin Has the Toni?' " *Union Leader* (July 1, 1963), p. 1.

60. "Forgive Us, Your Majesty," *Union Leader* (November 13, 1963), p. 1.

Leader inaugurated the new year with a three-part series by reporter D. Frank O'Neil, "Report from Rocky's Backyard,"[61] which painted an unflattering picture of Rockefeller's allegedly sloppy and spendthrift administration in New York.

The divorce-remarriage matter continued to be a main theme throughout the primary campaign. A February 29th front-page editorial, "Kissing Comes Easy to Gov. Rockefeller," added a foreign-policy angle by displaying a large photograph of Rockefeller about to embrace Nikita Khrushchev. Loeb also regularly attacked the Governor's "me-too" Republicanism and argued that Goldwater had a better chance to win in November.

According to my analysis of the *Union Leader* "sample pages" (the first three pages, the back page, and the editorial page), from January 1, 1964, through March 10 (the day of the primary election), the newspaper carried 109 "positive" or "neutral" stories about Goldwater and 50 about Rockefeller; one clearly unfavorable story about Goldwater and 24 about Rockefeller; 26 photographs of Goldwater and 19 of Rockefeller, the latter including five clearly uncomplimentary photos; and 80 editorials favoring Goldwater, attacking Rockefeller, or both. An all-out effort!

Goldwater barely edged Rockefeller in the New Hampshire primary,[62] but both men were surprisingly outpolled by the write-in campaign for Henry Cabot Lodge.

Loeb's enthusiasm for Goldwater did not wane after the Senator won the Republican nomination. The *Union Leader* continued to boost Goldwater in the most enthusiastic terms while frequently blasting President Lyndon B. Johnson and his Great Society program. Goldwater, however, was smothered in the general election, as Johnson won 64 percent of the New Hampshire vote.

Throughout most of the second half of 1967 Loeb was not sure whether he favored Nixon or Ronald Reagan for the 1968 Republican presidential nomination, though the publisher finally came down on the side of Nixon. But Loeb knew from an early date whom he did *not* want to be president: Governor George Romney.

61. December 31, 1963, and January 2 and 3, 1964.
62. As in the rest of this section, I am referring to the presidential preference voting—not to the separate balloting for convention delegates.

From the middle of 1967 through autumn, the *Leader* served up
a concentrated dose of anti-Romney medicine. Loeb jumped on
Romney's personal characteristics, accusing him of being intellec-
tually incapable, of having an abrasive personality, and of being
less than honest.

In December the paper tuned its anti-Romney campaign to a
low pitch. Perhaps Loeb and his associates figured Romney was so
far behind in the polls that he was not worth attacking. Nevertheless, the paper's editorial approach to the Republican primary
continued to be more heavily anti-Romney than pro-Nixon. When
Romney gave up his hopeless cause and withdrew from the race
about two weeks before the election, Nixon was left without serious opposition and swept to a lopsided victory.

On the Democratic side, Loeb made it clear that he detested the
Vietnam views of Senator Eugene McCarthy. One week after Mc-
Carthy announced his primary candidacy in early January 1968,
Loeb wrote: "Whether Sen. McCarthy knows it or not, those
speeches of his are written in blood—not HIS blood, but the blood
of American boys who are killed because this war is prolonged by
those speeches."[63] Despite a few sharp anti-McCarthy editorials
(especially during the last week of the primary campaign), the
Leader did not launch a vigorous, sustained attack against Mc-
Carthy. Perhaps the editors did not consider him to be a very powerful candidate. Moreover, Loeb looked with disfavor on President
Johnson's domestic policies and his refusal to go all-out to "win"
the Vietnam conflict. In the end McCarthy won a moral victory
by barely losing to Johnson in the primary.

Focusing its attention on state races, the *Union Leader* did not
editorialize extensively about the 1968 presidential general election campaign. Loeb endorsed Nixon even though the publisher's
political views more closely approximated the positions of third-
party candidate George C. Wallace than those of either major party
nominee. Loeb argued that Wallace was taking votes from Nixon
and aiding Humphrey.[64]

63. "Addressed to Democrats Only," *Union Leader* (January 12, 1968), p. 1.
64. "A Vote for Wallace Is a Vote for HHH," *Union Leader* (September 17,
1968), p. 1.

In the November election Nixon took New Hampshire with 52 percent of the vote, with Humphrey winning 44 percent and Wallace only 4 percent.

Loeb's favorable attitude toward Nixon weakened and reversed as the President developed his conciliatory policy toward Mainland China. In an August 1971 editorial Loeb sharply attacked the new China policy and concluded with these words:

> This newspaper and its publisher therefore regretfully announce that if the Democrats—or any other political party with a prospect of capturing the White House—nominate a presidential candidate who is dedicated to the restoration of our national defenses and who is prepared to support a foreign policy designed to preserve the security and honor of the United States, we will support that candidate against President Nixon in the 1972 elections.[65]

Loeb found such a candidate several months later when conservative Representative John Ashbrook announced that he would challenge President Nixon for the Republican nomination. Emphasizing the anticommunist foreign policy theme, the *Union Leader* gave Ashbrook favorable news coverage and editorial support while continuing to criticize Nixon. The paper paid little attention to the liberal Republican candidate, Representative Paul McCloskey, though several editorial barbs were directed at him. From the day after the news of Ashbrook's entry through primary election day—December 31, 1971, through March 7, 1972—the *Leader's* key display pages carried 49 positive or neutral stories or photographs of Ashbrook and only 16 of McCloskey. Enjoying his incumbency status and basking in the publicity of his China trip, President Nixon received 101 non-negative stories and photos during this period. However, the *Leader* also published 14 clearly unfavorable stories about him, only one about McCloskey, and none about Ashbrook. At the same time the paper printed 34 editorials praising Ashbrook or attacking his opponents. Nixon easily won the primary with 68 percent of the vote, while McCloskey polled 20 percent and Ashbrook mustered only 10 percent.

65. "A Sad Good-Bye to an Old Friend," *Union Leader* (August 6, 1971), p. 1.

For once Loeb had found a Democratic candidate he could support in that party's 1972 presidential primary. Los Angeles Mayor Sam Yorty's conservative, anticommunist, anti-establishment political views and his colorful personality made him a natural recipient of Loeb's support. Perhaps Yorty was lightly regarded nationally and politically unknown in New Hampshire; undaunted, Loeb set out to make Yorty a household word as soon as he announced his candidacy on November 16, 1971. From the day after the news of Yorty's announcement (November 18) until primary election day (March 7), the *Leader's* "sample pages" carried 71 stories and 38 photographs of Yorty, along with 14 editorials supporting him. Some of the coverage apparently was designed to appeal to Manchester's Irish and Franco-American voters—such as a story and photo about Yorty visiting his mother's home village in Ireland,[66] and a photo of Yorty receiving the award of Knight of the Legion of Honor from French Prime Minister Jacques Chaban-Delmas.[67]

It was no secret that Loeb opposed one of the main Democratic candidates, Senator George McGovern. In a vein similar to his treatment of Eugene McCarthy in 1968, early in 1971 Loeb labeled McGovern "dangerous to the safety and security of this nation. . . . Furthermore, we consider Senator McGovern to be *personally* responsible for the deaths of thousands of American boys."[68] Nevertheless, *Union Leader* editorials virtually ignored McGovern during the primary campaign.

Rather, Loeb fixed his aim on Senator Edmund S. Muskie, the apparent front-runner. The *Leader* hit Muskie with frequent critical editorials and unfavorable news stories. Loeb portrayed Muskie as an unreliable opportunist who liked to switch his stands on a variety of issues—and as a somewhat unstable individual who could not be trusted with the nuclear button. Loeb aroused Muskie's anger by reprinting a *Newsweek* item that was unfavorable to his wife and by publishing a letter alleging that Muskie had made an ethnic slur against Franco-Americans. (This letter was later linked

66. "The Place Yorty Loves Best," *Union Leader* (January 28, 1972), p. 3.
67. Photograph, *Union Leader* (February 1, 1972), p. 30.
68. "Senator McGovern's Political Waterloo," *Union Leader* (February 25, 1971), p. 1.

with the Nixon Administration's "dirty tricks" operation.) On February 26 Muskie mounted a platform outside the *Leader*'s offices in Manchester to answer Loeb but broke down in the famous crying incident which is widely credited with having dealt a severe blow to his campaign.[69]

From January 6—when all major Democratic candidates had announced—through primary day on March 7, the key display pages of the *Union Leader* carried 60 positive or neutral stories and photos of Yorty, 42 of Muskie, 18 of McGovern, and 18 of Senator Vance Hartke. These "sample pages" also carried 15 clearly unfavorable stories about Muskie, two about McGovern, one about Hartke, and none about Yorty. During this same period 28 editorials appeared supporting Yorty or attacking his opponents; their dominant tone was anti-Muskie.

The Senator from Maine won the primary with 46 percent of the votes cast, but this showing was far below the performance hoped for by Muskie supporters. McGovern polled 37 percent, and Yorty came in a distant third with 6 percent.

However unhappy Loeb may have been with Nixon in the spring, there was little doubt about whom the publisher would select when confronted with the choice between the President and McGovern in the general election campaign. Giving Nixon his back-handed endorsement in July, Loeb wrote:

> The McGovern push is the main drive for power in the United States by the Communist Party. . . . even if you have to hold your nose to vote for President Nixon—and this newspaper has told its readers many times that we disagree with him on some issues—he is infinitely better than the wild man from South Dakota, who believes in surrender, abortion and pot.[70]

The *Union Leader* poured forth similar anti-McGovern material throughout the campaign, as Loeb concentrated on McGovern's

69. For a description of this incident and the *Union Leader* coverage of Muskie during the campaign, see Jules Witcover, "William Loeb and the New Hampshire Primary: A Question of Ethics," *Columbia Journalism Review*, 11 (1972), 14-25.

70. "The McGovern Plot," *Union Leader* (July 14, 1972), p. 1.

foreign policy views and attacked him from the standpoint of a "Social Issue"[71] conservative concerned about such problems as crime, drugs, and permissiveness. The paper went lightly on pro-Nixon material in favor of the anti-McGovern appeals. In the November election Nixon swamped McGovern in New Hampshire by a margin of almost two to one.

Among the various conclusions from the foregoing summary is that in presidential campaigns foreign-policy matters are more salient for Loeb than domestic issues. Certainly the *Union Leader* is concerned about domestic problems, especially those relating to the many-faceted "Social Issue." But in judging presidential candidates, Loeb devotes more attention to foreign policy. A candidate who does not advocate a strong, aggressive defense and foreign policy runs the danger of being attacked for softness on communism or worse—witness especially McCarthy and McGovern.

Presidential candidates strongly opposed by Loeb are almost invariably pictured as being deceitful and untrustworthy. And Loeb is eager to use the "spoiled rich boy" class appeal if the candidate he opposes comes from a wealthy family.

Another conclusion is that Loeb has been unsuccessful at convincing a majority of the electorate to support his candidate in presidential primaries. Or to turn this statement around, the *Union Leader* publisher does not hesitate to endorse candidates with little chance of winning. Besides Nixon in 1968 (whose main opponent withdrew before the primary election), the only three candidates endorsed by Loeb between 1960 and 1972 have failed to win the New Hampshire presidential primary: Goldwater in 1964, Ashbrook and Yorty in 1972. Of course, these candidates may have received more votes than they would have without *Union Leader* support.

In an attempt to detect possible *Union Leader* impact on the electorate, let us examine the correlations between the paper's circulation and voting for Loeb-endorsed candidates in presidential primaries and general elections between 1960 and 1972 (all four general-election endorsements went to Republicans). In addition,

71. Richard M. Scammon and Ben J. Wattenberg, *The Real Majority* (New York: Coward, McCann and Geoghegan, 1971), chapter 3.

Table 7

Union Leader Circulation and Voting in Presidential Primaries
and General Elections, 1960 to 1972 (for counties)

Primary Elections		*General Elections*	
	Product-		*Product-*
Candidate,	*Moment*	*Candidate,*	*Moment*
Year, Party	*Correlation*	*Year*	*Correlation*
Fisher, 1960 Dem.*	.22	Nixon, 1960	−.26
Goldwater, 1964 Rep.	.84	Goldwater, 1964	.33
Nixon, 1968 Rep.	.50	Nixon, 1968	.16
Johnson, 1968 Dem.*	.41	Nixon, 1972	.53
Ashbrook, 1972 Rep.	.44		
Yorty, 1972 Dem.	.87		

*Not endorsed by the *Union Leader.*

Table 7 includes the correlations for two primary candidates who
were not endorsed by Loeb but whose opponents (John Kennedy
and McCarthy) were frequently attacked by Loeb.

Especially noteworthy for the primaries are the spectacularly
strong correlations for Goldwater and Yorty. Perhaps the *Union
Leader* support for the Senator from Arizona—the most ardent
Loeb crusade in any of the presidential primaries—had a pronounced impact on Republican voters. The high correlation value
for Yorty suggests that the newspaper may be especially influential in the case of relatively unknown candidates; earlier in the
chapter I made the same speculation with regard to Harrison
Thyng and Meldrim Thomson. On the other hand, we might expect the Ashbrook correlation to have been stronger if the *Union
Leader* is especially influential for political newcomers. And we
should remember that neither Yorty nor Ashbrook obtained more
than 10 percent of the vote, so the apparent *Leader* influence did
not pay off in victory for Loeb's candidate.

Although few of the correlations are spectacular, *Leader* impact
could be important in presidential primaries even if the paper is

unable to determine the winner. In recent years the *margin* of victory (or percentage of the total vote for the winning candidate) has been almost as important as who actually won. Lyndon Johnson and Edmund Muskie "won" their respective primaries, but they were generally judged to have been the losers because their margins of victory failed to match preprimary expectations. Thus the *Leader* can be important if it is able to reduce the margins of some candidates; and Loeb may have done just that in the case of Muskie.

Turning to the general elections, we note the same movement in the positive direction from 1960 to 1972 that we observed in Table 2. The Goldwater correlation seems a bit high for the mid 60's, however—higher than for the 1964 Republican gubernatorial candidate (see the Table 2 value). Perhaps the Goldwater figure indicates at least a small amount of *Union Leader* impact in the 1964 presidential general election.

At first glance the 1972 correlation for Nixon appears to be notably strong, but I think that this election was probably an exceptional case, in the sense that McGovern was an unusually weak candidate in the *Leader's* most concentrated circulation area. The substantial correlation value for Nixon (which can also be viewed as a negative value for McGovern) may thus have been higher than usual even if the *Leader* exerted no influence.

There are good reasons for expecting the *Union Leader* to be unimportant in presidential general elections, since the voters obtain so much more information from the national news media than they do in gubernatorial and senatorial elections. Even in presidential primaries substantial coverage is provided by the Boston television stations. If we assume that the *Leader* has little or no impact in presidential primaries and general elections, the Table 7 correlations are due to factors other than the paper's influence. If that is the case, the causal interpretation of the gubernatorial and senatorial data is even more doubtful than I indicated earlier in this chapter, for if the presidential correlations are spurious, we expect the gubernatorial and senatorial correlations to follow the same pattern of spuriousness. Once again we must beware of facile conclusions.

Some Strategic Considerations

Even if our relationships purporting to demonstrate *Union Leader*
impact on the electorate are partially or totally spurious, New
Hampshire politicians *perceive* the newspaper's influence to be real
in gubernatorial and senatorial elections. Although they do not see
things exactly in terms of our quantitative measures, candidates
and their advisers notice similar variations; for example, candidates
supported strongly by the *Union Leader* tend to do well in Manchester, whereas those opposed by Loeb tend to run more poorly
in the paper's home city. Significant voter impact by the *Leader*
seems to be an unquestioned axiom among New Hampshire politicians. But even if some candidates are not absolutely certain that
apparent Loeb impact is actually real, the safest course is to hedge
one's bets and to act as if the paper really is powerful with the
electorate.

Thus there is an important link between this chapter's data and
earlier chapters which discussed candidates' strategies. As long as
the *Union Leader appears* to exert a significant impact on voters, it
will continue to be an important influence on campaign strategies.

One key element is still missing from this discussion. For either
basic dependent variable measuring performance by *Leader*-
endorsed candidates—the vote in the Manchester city zone compared with the rest of New Hampshire, and the vote in the
counties—the most important factor is how strongly the candidate
runs in the Manchester area. But another vital consideration is the
fraction of the total state vote contributed by Manchester and
suburbs. As noted in Chapter 1, for recent elections the Manchester city zone accounts for somewhat more than one third of the
vote in Democratic gubernatorial or senatorial primaries, somewhat more than one tenth in Republican primaries, and somewhat
less than one fifth of the vote in general elections. Therefore, if
politicians assume that the *Union Leader* significantly influences
its readers, we would expect Democratic primary candidates to be
the most careful about antagonizing the newspaper. It seems more
likely and more reasonable for candidates in Republican primaries
and general elections to defy Loeb; but even these politicians think
very carefully before incurring the wrath of the *Union Leader*.

CHAPTER SIX

Conclusions

This study has approached the Manchester *Union Leader* as a newspaper that appears to have great potential for influencing candidates and voters in statewide election campaigns. After a summary of the main findings, I shall discuss some broader implications.

Summary of Main Findings

In some cases the *Union Leader* has influenced the decisions of potential candidates to run or not to run. The anticipation of *Union Leader* support in a campaign has probably encouraged some politicians to run rather than to stay on the sidelines, as they might have done in the absence of the newspaper. Personal persuasion by Loeb and other *Union Leader* personnel has apparently played a part in such positive recruitment. On the other hand, it is highly likely that other potential candidates who felt that they needed Loeb's backing in order to make a strong race have decided not to run when they found that the publisher intended to support another candidate. Interviewees' opinions suggest that another kind of negative recruitment impact by Loeb has operated by discouraging the entry of potential candidates who have not wanted to subject themselves to the personal abuse of Loeb's stinging editorials.

In general the *Union Leader* is a significant influence on the campaign strategies of gubernatorial and senatorial candidates. It may be worth while to recall this 1967 statement by an experienced Democratic adviser: "You take a good, hard look at any major political campaign in the state of New Hampshire over the past ten or fifteen years, and you will find that the strategy of each one of those campaigns was designed very much with Mr. Loeb in mind."[1]

1. Interview, not for attribution, September 28, 1967.

Candidates do not always make decisions different from the actions
they would have chosen if they had not taken the *Leader* into
account. But almost all (if not all) major statewide candidates
anticipate Loeb's future actions in formulating their strategies.

The 1966 senatorial case provided two striking examples of the
paper's strategic impact—on William R. Johnson in the Republican
primary and Thomas J. McIntyre in the general election. Johnson's
entire campaign was organized around the goal of generating a
counterforce to the Loeb press. McIntyre's dominant campaign
theme was to attack Loeb and his connection with Republican
candidate Harrison R. Thyng. The 1966 case is a good illustration
of the *Leader's* impact not only on "content" strategies (the content of appeals to the electorate), but also on "method" strategies
(the method or communications channels used to transmit appeals
to the electorate). At the same time, we should recognize that
1966 was an unusual case conducive to the use of the anti-Loeb
strategy, because of the nature of General Thyng as a candidate.

The *Union Leader* influences candidates' handling of issues,
especially candidates trying to attract conservative voters or attempting to win Loeb's support. It is risky to assert that some
politicians have actually changed their *positions* on issues because
of the *Union Leader*, but it is safer to suggest that candidates'
emphasis on issues (which items to stress and which matters to
downplay) has been shaped by the newspaper. It is interesting to
note that all fifteen of the paper's endorsements in gubernatorial
primaries and general elections from 1960 to 1972 went to candidates who pledged to veto a general sales or income tax if elected.
By raising the veto-pledge question and giving it generous publicity,
the *Union Leader* has created an incentive for some candidates to
take the pledge and to emphasize that promise in their campaigning. At the same time, other candidates inclined to favor new taxation have probably refrained from taking this stand in public in
order to avoid *Union Leader* attacks.

In analyzing why the *Union Leader* exerts an impact on candidates' strategies, I have argued that an extremely important influence base of the newspaper is the belief by politicians that the
Loeb press influences voters. In turn this belief is based on the
observed relationship between *Leader* support and voting patterns

for candidates in a number of elections. Moreover, the perceived electoral impact of the paper is buttressed by the dominance of its circulation and the vigor of its political advocacy (in both editorials and news columns). Besides perceived voter impact, the second main influence base is the candidates' desires to avoid Loeb's vitriolic personal attacks.

A facilitating condition for the operation of the other influence bases is the fact that the *Union Leader* is widely read by politicians. These men read Loeb's paper because they think it is influential and because it contains the most complete news coverage of New Hampshire politics. Thus the extensiveness of *Leader* news coverage should be added to its circulation strength and its vigorous advocacy as characteristics that aid the paper's impact on politicians. Another facilitating condition is the paucity of New Hampshire television stations, a factor which increases the relative importance of newspapers for political communication.

One result of the *Leader's* impact on candidates is the important role the paper plays in helping to set the campaign agenda. That is, the Loeb press is one factor in determining what issues are discussed during a campaign, and on what terms. In this context I have labeled two closely related processes "issue initiation" and "issue definition." Through its impact on candidates' strategic calculations, the *Union Leader* has been able to raise and sustain some topics of campaign discussion (e.g., the tax issue in gubernatorial contests). One technique used by the newspaper to achieve this result has been consistently to define a complex issue in a certain way (e.g., by defining the tax-change issue as the "sales tax issue," the "broad-base tax issue," or the "pledge-to-veto issue" rather than the "tax-reform issue" or some other label calling attention to increased state expenditures).

Although the causal interpretation of the evidence is unclear, in general the data are consistent with the hypothesis that the *Union Leader* exerts considerable influence on the electorate. In gubernatorial and senatorial primaries from 1960 to 1972, candidates more intensively supported by the *Leader* in news coverage and editorials ran more strongly in the Manchester area compared with the rest of New Hampshire; the same conclusion is true of the general-election candidates of either party. Furthermore, in single primaries Loeb-supported candidates do better in the counties with higher *Leader* circulation; analogous influence is evident in general elections when the impact of party identification on voting patterns is taken into account.

Though not very strong evidence, several bits of data support the proposition that the *Union Leader* has the most voter impact in the cases of relatively unknown candidates. Likewise, there are tentative indications that *Leader* impact on the electorate may have been increasing over time.

It is plausible that the *Union Leader* has influenced the outcomes of four gubernatorial or senatorial primaries between 1960 and 1972: the victories by Wesley Powell (1960 Republican gubernatorial primary), Harrison R. Thyng (1966 Republican senatorial primay), Roger J. Crowley, Jr. (1970 Democratic gubernatorial primary), and Meldrim Thomson, Jr. (1972 Republican gubernatorial primary)—about one third of the primaries in which Loeb endorsed a candidate. In other words, if the *Leader* had not vigorously supported these candidates, their opponents may well have won.

As for gubernatorial and senatorial general elections from 1960 to 1972, the only contest which the *Union Leader* might have decided was Thomson's triumph in 1972. In one or two other instances, however, Loeb may have indirectly contributed to the outcome of a general election by helping to nominate a weak candidate (in which case the publisher's efforts backfired) or by fanning the flames of a bitter primary battle and thus weakening the party for the general election.

Circulation and voting patterns are consistent with the assertion that the *Union Leader* has influenced the New Hampshire electorate in the state's first-in-the nation presidential preference primaries. Although Loeb has supported few winners, he may have helped to destroy the candidacies of Romney in 1968 and Muskie in 1972. It is also arguable that he severely hurt Rockefeller in 1964.

Whether or not the *Union Leader* influence on the electorate is real, New Hampshire politicians perceive the connection as valid. This perception is vital for continued *Leader* impact on candidates' strategies.

Some Broader Implications

The kinds of *Union Leader* impact discussed above may very well operate in decision-making arenas other than election campaigns. *Leader* influence on the agenda of campaign discussion may be relatively unimportant for affecting election outcomes; but agenda-setting during campaigns might help to shape the agenda of state government between campaigns.[2] For instance, promises made by candidates during elections might help set priorities for the government after the campaign is over.

Even if campaign agenda have little influence on governmental agenda, the *Union Leader* might shape the agenda of New Hampshire state government between electon campaigns. The processes of issue initiation and issue definition may operate to induce official decision-makers to act on some matters. Setting the political agenda through the initiation and definition of issues is a subtle, hidden process but a very important one. E. E. Schattschneider wrote:

> Political conflict is not like an intercollegiate debate in which the opponents agree in advance on a definition of the issues. As a matter of fact, *the definition of the alternatives is the supreme instrument of power;* the antagonists can rarely agree on what the issues are because power is involved in the definition. He who determines what politics is about runs the country, because the definition of the alternatives is the choice of conflicts, and the choice of conflicts allocates power.[3]

If some issues or conflicts are included on the governmental agenda, the other side of the coin is that alternative topics of discussion are omitted. Perhaps the *Union Leader* plays a nondecision-making[4] role in helping to keep some issues off the governmental

2. For a systematic analysis of political agendas, see Robert W. Cobb and Charles D. Elder, *Participation in American Politics: The Dynamics of Agenda-Building* (Boston: Allyn and Bacon, 1972).

3. E. E. Schattschneider, *The Semisovereign People* (New York: Holt, Rinehart and Winston, 1960), p. 68. (Author's italics.)

4. Peter Bachrach and Morton S. Baratz, *Power and Poverty* (New York: Oxford University Press, 1970).

agenda. Or if these topics are included, they may be defined in such a way as to benefit one side of the dispute at the expense of the opposing side. Along with other factors, the *Leader* may focus serious political debate on the question of additional taxes while deflecting meaningful attention from possible new governmental programs in such areas as education, housing, and health care. The *Leader* may share some of the credit for New Hampshire's regressive tax structure and the absence of a general sales or income tax.

A number of interviewees assert that the *Leader* significantly influences members of the New Hampshire Legislature (the General Court), especially members from the large Manchester delegation. From time to time *Leader* editorials carry the names of legislators who have voted "wrong" on bills considered important by the newspaper.

Along with the Concord *Monitor*, the *Union Leader* is a widely read source of political information in the state capital. Speaking in 1972 during Governor Peterson's administration, *Monitor* political editor and reporter Rod Paul related:

> If it's a slow day and I happen to wander into the Governor's office and he's there—he's just arrived or something—there he is, looking at the *Union Leader*, shaking his head and "Ah, look what they did with this," or "Look what they did with that." Or if I go up to the House Speaker's office, more often than not: "Did you see what the *Union Leader* did with that today?" "Yeah, well that's the latest scene. All right, we'll deal with it this way in the Legislature."[5]

Particularly if he is a fairly cautious person whose political position is not on the liberal side of the spectrum, an elected official may hesitate to take actions that would stimulate bitter *Union Leader* criticism. Several interviewees suggest that the newspaper's influence is not confined to state officials but may extend to some members of New Hampshire's congressional delegation as well. It would be highly risky to attribute any political change over time to the *Union Leader*, but it is a fact that Congressmen Louis C. Wyman and James C. Cleveland have become more acceptable to

5. Interview with Rod Paul, August 25, 1972.

Loeb since their arrival in Washington in 1962. Endorsing Wyman and Cleveland for reelection in 1968, Loeb wrote:

> This newspaper has criticized Louis Wyman IN THE PAST for the fact that his good looks and personal charm had not been equalized by good judgment and perseverance. But, the passage of time, as it does frequently, has improved Louis and he has much more common sense nowadays. . . .
> In the second district, we have Congressman Cleveland. While he was a member of the State Senate, Mr. Cleveland made a number of attacks against this newspaper and was among the wildest liberals and bleeding hearts that had ever come along.
> But Congressman Cleveland apparently has realized that he represents a rather conservative constituency in his district and he has turned into a much more sensible congressman and a much better human being. He deserves reelection.[6]

Union Leader impact might also operate in a wide variety of settings outside the formal institutions of government. One possibility is the board of trustees of the University of New Hampshire. Or another example: in 1969 newly inaugurated Governor Peterson appointed a Citizens' Task Force (dubbed the "Citizens' Tax Farce" by the *Union Leader*) to study and make recommendations on a variety of problems facing the state. A member of a Task Force subcommittee recalls:

> [Besides the subcommittee chairman] there wasn't anybody else who had any political—at least no obvious political ambitions, and certainly no real political connections. And yet even in a situation where citizens were supposed to be looking at issues, there was a theme of what the Manchester *Union Leader* might do; this was a recurring theme in our discussions. . . . And so I think the people who considered themselves more realistic and practical may have been influenced in their final evaluation of the program by what they thought might be least offensive to the *Union Leader*.[7]

6. "Almost 'No Contest,' " *Union Leader* (November 2, 1968), p. 1.
7. Interview with Charles F. Leahy, August 23, 1972.

It appears that anticipation of possible future actions by the *Union Leader* certainly is not confined to the electoral arena.

Another hypothesis is that the *Union Leader* is able to confer legitimacy or illegitimacy (acceptability or unacceptability) on certain political positions. Perhaps the Loeb press acts as a deterrent to the open expression of opinions opposed by the newspaper. The dislike of personal attack by the paper may operate outside election campaigns. Reflecting an opinion stated by several other interviewees, former Governor Peterson asserts:

> I think that the big thing that the *Union Leader* has done in New Hampshire is created something of a climate of fear with many people—so that lots of leaders in the state won't speak out for fear of being pilloried in the pages of the *Union Leader*. There's a kind of an attitude that "Well, I'm against them and don't like what they're doing, but I can't speak out because it might hurt my business or might damage a hopeful political career," or some such thing.[8]

Whether speaking of election campaigns or other arenas, we should beware of ignoring the environment in which the *Union Leader* operates. In stating that the newspaper produces a certain effect, we should not forget the contextual variables that make that impact possible—for example, the receptivity of the audience or the relative weakness of competing communications media. Moreover, the *Leader's* impact may be not direct but mediated through other factors. For example, the newspaper might facilitate the exercise of influence by organizations of conservative candidates in campaigns.

What are the implications of the New Hampshire case for other parts of the United States? We might expect that newspapers in other places have the kinds of impact exerted by the *Union Leader* to the extent that these media are characterized by dominance of circulation and vigorous political advocacy. Not many other newspapers enjoy the *Leader's* position as the newspaper with the greatest circulation, but the Loeb press is certainly not unique. One measure of relative circulation strength is the per-

8. Interview with Walter Peterson, December 8, 1972.

centage of total daily newspaper circulation in a state accounted for by a given paper; according to this indicator and 1972 circulation data, papers in seventeen other states have at least as dominant a circulation position as the *Union Leader*. A second measure of dominance is the circulation ratio of the largest to the second-largest newspaper in a state; according to this indicator, papers in thirteen other states are at least as dominant as the *Leader*. Newspapers in nineteen states equal or surpass the *Leader* on either of the two measures.[9] Thus the paper is not an especially rare case in terms of circulation strength. However, the Loeb press may be more nearly unique with respect to the minimal impact of New Hampshire television.

Besides circulation dominance, vigorous political advocacy is the second hypothesized requisite for newspaper impact. Here there is good reason to doubt the relevance of the *Leader* case outside New Hampshire. The constant conscious and blatant use of news coverage as a vehicle for political advocacy is rarely employed to the extent that it is by the *Leader*. Loeb's strong personal attacks on politicians are another rarity; thus, we would expect few other papers to benefit from candidates' desires to avoid such criticism. Vigorous newspaper advocacy does not imply vitriolic personal attacks or the espousal of an extreme political philosophy, however, and attempts at political persuasion confined entirely to editorials and devoid of personal assaults can have a significant impact on voters and candidates—especially if the editorials are occasionally placed on the front page.

In sum the usefulness of the *Union Leader* as a general case is limited. If other newspapers exerting impact similar to that of the *Leader* exist, they can probably be found as newspaper monopolies in urban politics or large papers in congressional districts.

Basically, this study has demonstrated the *potential* power inherent in the control of a dominant communications medium in a political entity.

9. Calculated from 1972 circulation figures published in the *Editor and Publisher International Year Book*, 1973. The calculations assume that all the copies of a newspaper published in a state circulate in that state. However, the circulation of the Lebanon-White River Junction *Valley News* has been split between New Hampshire and Vermont, as explained in Chapter 3.

Appendixes

Appendix A

New Hampshire Election Results for Major Offices, 1960–1972

(Note: Contests with only one candidate receiving more than 10 percent of the total vote are omitted. For the included races, the votes of only those candidates receiving at least 10 percent of the total vote are listed; but the percentages are based on the total number of votes cast.)

GENERAL ELECTIONS

President
Richard M. Nixon (R)   157,989 (53%)
Kennedy (D)   137,772 (47%)

Governor
Powell* (R)   161,123 (55%)
Boutin (D)   129,404 (45%)

Senator
Styles Bridges,* (Concord (R)   173,521 (60%)
Hill (D)   114,024 (40%)

Congressman: CD 1
Merrow* (R)   88,118 (57%)
Champagne (D)   67,717 (43%)

Congressman: CD 2
Bass* (R)   77,701 (60%)
Stuart V. Nims, Keene (D)   51,145 (40%)

PRIMARIES

1960

Presidential Preference (Dem.)
John F. Kennedy   43,372 (85%)
Paul C. Fisher   6,853 (13%)

Governor (Dem.)
Bernard L. Boutin, Laconia   31,650 (78%)
John Shaw, Rochester   7,151 (18%)

Governor (Rep.)
Wesley Powell,* Hampton Falls   49,119 (50%)
Hugh Gregg, Nashua   48,108 (49%)

Senator (Dem.)
Herbert W. Hill, Hanover   16,198 (40%)
Alphonse Roy, Manchester   13,782 (34%)
Frank L. Sullivan, Manchester   10,266 (26%)

Congressman: CD 1 (Dem.)
Romeo J. Champagne, Manchester   19,124 (72%)
Joseph R. Myers, Manchester   7,412 (28%)

Congressman: CD 1 (Rep.)
Chester E. Merrow,* Ossipee   33,183 (66%)
Norman A. Packard, Manchester   16,730 (34%)

Congressman: CD 2 (Rep.)
Perkins Bass,* Peterborough   34,907 (80%)
Margaret B. Chandler, Warner   5,477 (13%)

1962

Governor (Rep.)
John Pillsbury, Manchester	55,784	(56%)
Wesley Powell,* Hampton Falls	42,005	(42%)

Senator: Short Term (Rep.)
Perkins Bass, Peterborough	31,037	(31%)
Doloris Bridges, Concord	29,345	(30%)
Maurice J. Murphy, Jr.,* Portsmouth	24,204	(24%)
Chester E. Merrow, Ossipee	14,417	(15%)

Congressman: CD 1 (Rep.)
Louis C. Wyman, Manchester	22,118	(44%)
George Gilman, Farmington	11,707	(23%)
Chester M. Wiggin, Jr., Conway	11,646	(23%)

Congressman: CD 2 (Dem.)
Eugene S. Daniell, Jr., Franklin	6,589	(74%)
Helen L. Bliss, Rindge	2,327	(26%)

Congressman: CD 2 (Rep.)
James C. Cleveland, New London	14,640	(33%)
Bert F. Teague, Newport	13,900	(31%)
Stacey W. Cole, Swanzey	6,100	(14%)
Paul A. Rinden, Concord	5,518	(12%)

Governor
John W. King, Manchester (D)	135,481	(59%)
Pillsbury (R)	94,567	(41%)

Senator: Short Term
Thomas J. McIntyre, Laconia (D)	117,612	(52%)
Bass (R)	107,199	(48%)

Senator: Full Term
Norris Cotton,* Lebanon (R)	134,035	(60%)
Alfred Catalfo, Jr., Dover (D)	90,444	(40%)

Congressman: CD 1
Wyman (R)	65,651	(53%)
J. Oliva Huot, Laconia (D)	57,910	(47%)

Congressman: CD 2
Cleveland (R)	56,152	(57%)
Daniell (D)	41,539	(42%)

(Continued)

*Incumbent.

PRIMARIES

1964

Presidential Preference (Rep.)

Henry Cabot Lodge	33,007	(36%)
Barry M. Goldwater	20,692	(22%)
Nelson A. Rockefeller	19,504	(21%)
Richard M. Nixon	15,587	(17%)

Governor (Rep.)

John Pillsbury, Manchester	32,200	(51%)
Wesley Powell, Hampton Falls	21,764	(35%)

Congressman: CD 1 (Dem.)

J. Oliva Huot, Laconia	12,275	(56%)
Charles F. Whittemore, Pembroke	9,499	(44%)

Congressman: CD 1 (Rep.)

Louis C. Wyman,* Manchester	28,534	(87%)
Charles Leonard Corbin, Laconia	4,171	(13%)

1966

Governor (Rep.)

Hugh Gregg, Nashua	33,946	(45%)
James J. Barry, Manchester	20,791	(27%)
Alexander M. Taft, Greenville	14,845	(20%)

GENERAL ELECTIONS

President

Lyndon B. Johnson* (D)	182,065	(64%)
Goldwater (R)	104,029	(36%)

Governor

John W. King,* Manchester	190,863	(67%)
Pillsbury (R)	94,824	(33%)

Congressman: CD 1

Huot (D)	79,097	(51%)
Wyman* (R)	74,939	(49%)

Congressman: CD 2

James C. Cleveland,* New London (R)	62,680	(50.1%)
Charles B. Officer, Claremont (D)	62,382	(49.9%)

Governor

John W. King,* Manchester (D)	125,882	(54%)
Gregg (R)	107,259	(46%)

Senator (Rep.)
Harrison R. Thyng, Barnstead 22,741 (30%)
Wesley Powell, Hampton Falls 18,145 (24%)
William R. Johnson, Hanover 17,410 (23%)
Lane Dwinell, Lebanon 10,781 (14%)
Doloris Bridges, Concord 7,613 (10%)

Senator
Thomas J. McIntyre,* Laconia (D) 123,888 (54%)
Thyng (R) 105,241 (46%)

Congressman: CD 1 (Dem.)
J. Oliva Huot,* Laconia 14,186 (77%)
William F. Horan, Jr., Manchester 4,255 (23%)

Congressman: CD 1 (Rep.)
Louis C. Wyman, Manchester 33,931 (84%)
Richard M. Schrader, Exeter 4,578 (11%)

Congressman: CD 1
Wyman (R) 72,869 (56%)
Huot* (D) 56,740 (44%)

Congressman: CD 2 (Dem.)
William H. Barry, Jr., Nashua 6,629 (67%)
Eugene S. Daniell, Jr., Franklin 3,240 (33%)

Congressman: CD 2
James C. Cleveland,* New London (R) 66,179 (67%)
Barry (D) 32,835 (33%)

1968

Presidential Preference (Dem.)
Lyndon B. Johnson* 27,520 (50%)
Eugene McCarthy 23,263 (42%)

Presidential Preference (Rep.)
Richard M. Nixon 80,666 (78%)
Nelson A. Rockefeller 11,241 (11%)

President
Nixon (R) 154,903 (52%)
Hubert H. Humphrey (D) 130,589 (44%)

(Continued)

PRIMARIES

1968, cont.

Governor (Dem.)
Emile R. Bussiere, Manchester	12,021	(33%)
Henry P. Sullivan, Manchester	10,895	(30%)
Vincent P. Dunn, Concord	10,412	(28%)

Governor (Rep.)
Walter Peterson, Peterborough	29,262	(34%)
Wesley Powell, Hampton Falls	26,498	(31%)
Meldrim Thomson, Jr., Oxford	25,275	(29%)

Congressman: CD 1 (Dem.)
James T. Keefe, Manchester	13,171	(65%)
William F. Horan, Jr., Manchester	7,137	(35%)

Congressman: CD 2 (Dem.)
David C. Hoeh, Hanover	6,888	(84%)
Henry P. Sullivan, Manchester	1,196	(15%)

1970

Governor (Dem.)
Roger J. Crowley, Jr., Manchester	17,089	(47%)
Charles F. Whittemore, Pembroke	13,354	(37%)

GENERAL ELECTIONS

Governor
Peterson (R)	149,902	(53%)
Bussiere (D)	135,378	(47%)

Senator
Norris Cotton,* Lebanon (R)	170,163	(59%)
John W. King, Goffstown (D)	116,816	(41%)

Congressman: CD 1
Louis C. Wyman,* Manchester (R)	100,269	(63%)
Keefe (D)	57,959	(37%)

Congressman: CD 2
James C. Cleveland,* New London (R)	88,609	(71%)
Hoeh (D)	35,942	(29%)

Dennis J. Sullivan, Nashua — 4,747 (13%)

Governor (Rep.)
Walter Peterson,* Peterborough — 43,667 (51%)
Meldrim Thomson, Jr., Orford — 41,392 (48%)

Congressman: CD 1 (Dem.)
Chester E. Merrow, Ossipee — 9,658 (51%)
William F. Horan, Jr., Manchester — 5,927 (31%)
Michael Dombroski, Newmarket — 3,453 (18%)

Congressman: CD 2 (Dem.)
Eugene S. Daniell, Jr., Franklin — 8,552 (64%)
Edward W. Gude, Orange — 4,770 (36%)

1972

Presidential Preference (Dem.)
Edmund S. Muskie — 41,235 (46%)
George S. McGovern — 33,007 (37%)

Presidential Preference (Rep.)
Richard M. Nixon* — 79,239 (68%)
Paul McCloskey — 23,190 (20%)
John Ashbrook — 11,362 (10%)

Governor (Dem.)
Roger J. Crowley, Manchester — 29,326 (61%)
Robert E. Raiche, Manchester — 16,216 (34%)

Governor
Peterson* (R) — 102,298 (46%)
Crowley (D) — 98,098 (44%)
Thomson (Am.) — 22,033 (10%)

Congressman: CD 1
Louis C. Wyman,* Manchester (R) — 72,170 (67%)
Merrow (D) — 34,882 (33%)

Congressman: CD 2
James C. Cleveland,* New London (R) — 74,219 (70%)
Daniell (D) — 32,374 (30%)

President
Nixon* (R) — 213,724 (64%)
McGovern (D) — 116,435 (35%)

(Continued)

PRIMARIES

1972, cont.

Governor (Rep.)
Meldrim Thomson, Jr., Oxford   43,611   (48%)
Walter Peterson,* Peterborough   41,252   (45%)

Senator (Rep.)
Wesley Powell, Hampton Falls   42,837   (48%)
Peter J. Booras, Keene   19,714   (22%)
David A. Brock, Manchester   16,326   (18%)
Marshall W. Cobleigh, Nashua   10,106   (11%)

Congressman: CD 1 (Dem.)
Chester E. Merrow, Ossipee   14,772   (59%)
Sylvia F. Chaplain, Bedford   10,093   (41%)

GENERAL ELECTIONS

Governor
Thomson (R)   133,702   (41%)
Crowley (D)   126,107   (39%)
Malcolm McLane, Concord (Ind.)   63,199   (20%)

Senator
Thomas J. McIntyre,* Laconia (D)   184,495   (57%)
Powell (R)   139,852   (43%)

Congressman: CD 1
Louis C. Wyman,* Manchester (R)   115,732   (73%)
Merrow (D)   42,996   (27%)

Congressman: CD 2
James C. Cleveland,* New London (R) 105,915   (68%)
Charles B. Officer, Hanover (D)   50,066   (32%)

Source: *State of New Hampshire Manual for the General Court*, 1961, 1963, 1965, 1967, 1969, 1971, and 1973 (Concord: Department of State).

Appendix B

The Nature and Treatment of the Interviews

Most of the interviews that form the basis of this study were conducted in the summer and fall of 1967. At that time top priority
was given to arranging interviews with recent candidates for major
statewide office or their campaign advisers. Preference was given
to candidates in gubernatorial and senatorial campaigns over congressional contests, to more recent campaigns over earlier races,
and to closer elections over more one-sided elections. Higher
priority was assigned to candidates than to campaign aides. I discovered, however, that these advisers were often more candid and
more insightful than candidates in the interviews. In addition, I
interviewed several political activists unconnected with any particular campaigns, as well as a number of newspapermen. Besides
the 60 formal interviews, I held informal discussions with politicians, journalists, and professors. Originally confining my inter-
viewing to New Hampshire, I later added several Vermont
interviews for comparative purposes.

In 1972 I returned to update the original study and conducted
17 more interviews on a very selective basis (all but two involved
New Hampshirities). In the following tabulations I have not counted
one of the more recent interviews with a person I had also interviewed in 1967.

Following are several categorizations of the 76 interviewees:

	New Hampshire	Vermont	Total
Candidates	23	9*	32*
Campaign managers and advisers	15	1	16
Other political activists	9	0	9
Newspaper publishers	3	1*	4*
Newspaper editors	5	3	8
Newspaper reporters	5	3	8
	60	17*	77*

*Includes one double-counted interviewee, who was both a candidate and a
newspaper publisher.

	Politicians Only New Hampshire	Vermont	Total
Party			
Democratic	23	5	28
Republican	23	5	28
Independent	1	0	1
	47	10	57

Office of (Most Recent) Campaign	Candidates and Advisers Only New Hampshire	Vermont	Total
Governor	13	7	20
Senator	16	0	16
Congressman	9	2	11
Other	0	1	1
	38	10	48

Outcome of (Most Recent) Campaign(s)	Candidates and Advisers Only New Hampshire	Vermont	Total
Won	10	2	12
Lost	20	4	24
Won Primary, Lost General Election	8	4	12
	38	10	48

Union Leader Editorial Position in (Most Recent) Campaign	New Hampshire Candidates and Advisers Only
Endorsed by Union Leader	7
Opposed by Union Leader	27
Union Leader neutral	4
	38

The predominance of candidates opposed by the *Union Leader* is not surprising, given a few multicandidate primaries in which the newspaper endorsed one aspirant while opposing several others.

All but five of the interviews were tape recorded. Before each interview I told the person that he would not be quoted for attribution unless he gave his permission to do so. Many of the interviewees immediately granted blanket permission to be quoted. A very small number asked not to be quoted for attribution. The remainder were later given the opportunity to delete attributed quotes from use in the study. It is my impression that most of the interviewees were candid and that the tape recorder did not inhibit responses. On the other hand, it is obvious that there are some matters the interviewees would not reveal, regardless of the presence or absence of a tape recorder. The average length of the interviews was about 45 minutes; several were conducted in two or more separate sessions.

Starting with a list of basic questions for the flexible, semi-structured interviews, I added other queries according to the individual experiences of the respondents. First I questioned the politicians about their own campaigns. If time permitted, I then asked about other campaigns and more general topics.

In a fundamental sense I treated the evidence uncovered in the interviews qualitatively rather than quantitatively. In some compelling respects the responses are not equal and averageable with one another. While the general quality of the interviewees is high, they vary widely in perceptiveness and insight into the relations between the mass media and political campaigns. Moreover, in some situations personal opinions are obviously biased by personal involvement in the subject being discussed. It would be misleading therefore, to attach the same weight to all opinions; the responses should not be treated as a number of equal statistical units. This observation is especially pertinent because the interviewees do not constitute a sample selected randomly from a larger universe (although I have no reason to believe that the respondents are in any important respect unrepresentative of recent statewide candidates). On the other hand, in several instances I used a limited quantitative approach to the extent of indicating whether the opinions on a question are virtually unanimous or whether a significant split occurs (if the minority view constitutes, say, one third or more of the expressed opinions).

One basic rule I followed in presenting the interview material was to include any views opposing an expressed opinion or interpretation. This practice guards against the danger of an overly one-sided presentation of the evidence, a process in which the author may ignore views which run counter to his own preconceptions.

Because of the absence of sophisticated quantification, most of the evidence from the interviews assumes a relatively "soft" appearance—at least compared with the "hard" statistical data in mass survey projects. This suggestive, qualitative evidence carries the disadvantage of not allowing generalizations confidently from a randomly selected sample to a well-defined universe. I believe, however, that the most important and theoretically significant forms of newspaper influence are the most difficult to quantify, even if extensive resources are available for research.

Appendix C

The Newspaper Content Analysis

A reading of newspapers was used to derive the news-story and editorial data employed in Chapter 5, and also to obtain background. Although I analyzed the Concord *Monitor*, Burlington *Free Press*, Rutland *Herald*, St. Albans *Messenger*, and Vermont *Sunday News* for some campaigns, only data from the Manchester *Union Leader* (including the New Hampshire *Sunday News*) were used in the final version of this study. The Loeb press was analyzed systematically from the beginning of 1960 through the end of 1972. My source was the microfilm files of Baker Library, Dartmouth College, Hanover, New Hampshire.

During the time period of a content analysis, I examined every issue of a newspaper, devoting particular attention to news stories and editorials about declared candidates for major office. For the purposes of the variables used in Chapter 5, "length of the campaign" is defined as the number of issues of a paper from the first day after news appeared of the announcements of the candidate supported editorially by the paper and at least one other candidate (or, if nobody was endorsed by the paper, from the first day after news of the announcements of any two candidates for the office) until election day.

For every issue of a newspaper I examined six pages: 1, 2, 3, the first page of the second section, the back page, and the editorial page (the *Union Leader*'s editorial page is the first page of the second section). Attention was restricted to these pages because it was not feasible to examine all pages of a large number of issues. In this connection I felt that it would be more productive to analyze a few pages of many issues rather than all of the pages of a few issues (the latter is the usual procedure in newspaper content analysis). Moreover, the pages selected for examination are the most prominent of a newspaper and therefore more likely to catch the attention of readers than the other inside pages.

Also because of time considerations, I read few complete stories about declared candidates: I classified them on the basis of headline content. This short-cut is valid insofar as headlines accurately summarize the content of the news stories or insofar as a large proportion of individuals read only headlines but not the stories themselves.

Each news story (headline) about a declared candidate was classified in one of two ways: (A) "positive" or "neutral" toward the candidate, or (B) "negative" toward the candidate. The distinction between these two categories is not sharp and often requires a subjective judgment to be made. The rule I followed was to classify a story as neutral if I felt that there was any reasonable doubt about the classification; I placed only stories that were clearly unfavorable toward a candidate in the negative category. The majority of negative stories were critical statements about a candidate made by somebody other than his opponent. I classified stories in which a candidate criticized his opponent as being positive-neutral for the candidate making the statement. Headlines containing the names of two candidates in a non-negative manner were counted twice, once for each candidate. I also noted photographs of candidates in the sample pages. These photos were almost always placed in the positive-neutral category, the rare exceptions occurring when a picture was obviously unflattering or when it was accompanied by a clearly unfavorable caption about the candidate.

The position of a story was recorded according to whether I judged it to be the most prominent on the page, the second or third most prominent, or just one of the other stories on the page. Later I assigned a series of arbitrary weights for story placement (for example, the lead story on page one counted six times as much as a small story on page two or three). Combining these values with weights for photographs, I derived a weighted news coverage score for each candidate. However, I did not use the weighted scores when I discovered they were virtually identical to the unweighted scores used for the news advantage variables in Chapter 5. For the ten Republican gubernatorial and senatorial primaries shown in Figure 1, the product-moment correlation between the weighted and unweighted News Advantage Scores is a near-perfect .97, and the analogous correlation for the thirteen general elections shown in Figure 3 is .98. Thus it makes no statistical difference whether the weighted or unweighted variables are used.

In contrast to news stories, I read the editorials about candidates in their entirety, classifying each editorial as positive or negative toward one of the candidates. An editorial positive toward one candidate and negative toward his opponent(s) was counted only once, as being positive for the favored politician. The few editorials favorable toward more than one candidate were counted more than once, one time for each of the congratulated candidates. Editorials which did not express a positive or negative opinion about at least one candidate were not tallied. I counted editorial cartoons in the same way as editorials. These notations formed the basis of the Editorial Support Score defined in Chapter 5.

I analyzed the morning State Edition of the *Union Leader*, which circulates throughout New Hampshire; the evening City Edition goes to the Manchester area. For the circulation-voting relationships for counties (Chapter 5), the State Edition is more appropriate. But for the content-voting relationships (the Manchester city zone vs. the rest of New Hampshire), the City Edition would be preferable. For my purposes, however, the two editions are virtually interchangeable, since their coverage of statewide political campaigns is so similar—at least in the sample pages. In order to confirm this similarity, I analyzed both the State and City editions from August 1 to August 29, 1972 (a total of 25 issues for each edition). Three major primary campaigns were in progress during this period. For the ten candidates running in these campaigns, the product-moment correlation between the number of State Edition news stories in the key display pages and the number of City Edition news stories in the sample pages is a very strong .95 (photographs are also included in these figures). The Editorial Support Scores for the three campaigns are identical for the two editions. Assuming that this pattern is repeated in other campaigns, the State and City editions are indeed interchangeable for the purposes of my analysis.

Index